issue three | 2020

NELLE

issue three | 2020

University of Alabama at Birmingham

NELLE is an annual publication open to submissions from any female-identifying writer. *NELLE* accepts original and unpublished poetry, fiction, and nonfiction between the January 1 and September 1 reading period. Complete submission guidelines are available on our online submission manager at https://nelle.submittable.com/submit. To subscribe and learn more visit https://www.uab.edu/cas/englishpublications/nelle. For any other correspondence, contact us at editors.nelle@gmail.com.

NELLE is a member of the Council of Literary Magazines and Presses (CLMP) and the Council of Editors of Learned Journals (CELJ). Indexed by the Humanities International Index and in Feminist Periodicals: A Current Listing of Contents.

NELLE is available for order through all bookstores and available online through major vendors.

Colophon: *NELLE* is printed using the font Dante MT for the text and Burford for displays.

Staff

editor-in-chief
Lauren Goodwin Slaughter

managing editor
Anamaria Santiago

assistant managing editor
Mandy Riggs

senior editors
Halley Cotton, Poetry

assistant editors
Taylor Byas
Shelly Cato
Kristin Entler
Emily Krawczyk
Scot Langland
Mandy Riggs

business manager
Karen Ann Coggin

intern and social media
Miranda Riggs

cover art
"St. Clair" by Debra Eubanks Riffe

production/printing
47 Journals, LLC

Contents

Contents

From the Editor

Dear Readers,

How would you describe that look staring back at you
from the cover of *NELLE,* issue three?
Those eyes: are they daring or summoning you? Is the gaze
one of protest or power?
Perhaps it's all of the above and more. Each inspection
of this stunning block print by Debra Eubanks Riffe reveals
something new; the way floral shapes within that doily gag
suggest howling, the dark flicks in the right eye. It's the same
with the writing in this issue—each piece wants your clear
attention. Look, they challenge. Look closer. I dare you.
We are privileged at *NELLE* to host The Three Sisters
Prizes, which the editors annually award to one work each
in the categories of poetry, fiction, and nonfiction. It was
especially difficult to make our selections this year. Our
choice in nonfiction, Virginia Bell's lyric essay, "Chicken,"
reflects on the contradictory elements of a father's identity,
especially regarding his sexuality. What does it mean to "come
out," Bell asks, and what does a lifelong game of "chicken"
look like? In "Jane Doe," our fiction recipient, Susan Taylor
Chehak, explores—against a seemingly ordinary Midwestern
landscape—the most brutal forms of female erasure for a
girl who seems to have lost everything, including her name.
Natasha Deonarain's poem, "Pretoria, South Africa, 1945,"
expresses moments of whimsy and beauty in a look at a
mother's white privilege and a multiracial daughter's struggle
under Apartheid. These works, along with many others in this
issue, engage with the themes suggested by the cover. Who
in our culture is permitted to speak and be visible? Whose
voices and bodies are systematically silenced or shamed? These
themes appear so persistently, it's almost as if we'd planned it

(we didn't). I could go on, but let's skip to the good part: the authors' own words.

Just one final note inspired by the cover art and by so many pieces in this issue: even muzzled, we can find holes through which to breathe. Or scream. Or sing.

Thanks, as always. Take care.

Yours,

Lauren Slaughter
Editor-in-chief

Francesca Bell

THE DENTIST SAYS IT'S FROM SOME EARLIER DAMAGE

In my head, a dead tooth
is lodged among the living
as I am lodged in this life.

How can I tell
one thing
from another?

How can I explain I feel
like the tooth feels
now that it doesn't?

Dead or alive,
it gleams
in every picture,

only faintly discolored.
I appear smiling
in every moment

at the center of the family
while I house
some real thing

in a state of slow decay.
The pulp in my tooth
has nearly calcified

NELLE

as I have nearly hardened
before the stove,
fixed, fastened,

a dead thing
no one realized
was dying.

I carry this tooth
in my mouth,
like a sentence

I cannot speak.

Francesca Bell

DUSK, THE DAY I DROVE MY CHILD TO THE PARTIAL HOSPITALIZATION PROGRAM

The trees' branched openwork is bare, exposed
by autumn's fretsaw. Color shines through
the blank spaces, color of days closing like doors,
one by one, against me.

I pause, having emptied *properly* my little bucket
of food scraps, and wheeled the trashcans, relieved
of their stinking loads, back in place, snug
against our house.

I think of how succulents compost their own bodies, hold water
in each thick leaf, sit tidy in pots I've placed carefully on my
clean-swept porch. And did I tell you how useless it all is
before the ravages

of the starved synapse? Even the bread I bake doesn't help,
despite its wild rising, its very fine crumb.
Orchids on their bright sill open reliably
their freckled faces.

No small feat, this reblooming, when too much care
is as dooming as too little. I do everything meticulously,
walk motherhood's narrow ledge, and still stand
watching light fade

through the oaks' snarled tracery, seeing it wane as the sky goes
from rose to pink to pale. It ends up black no matter,
the trees' outlines engulfed each night
by the dark.

Francesca Bell

DECIDUOUS

I want to be the tree
when cold has come,

after rain has run
like lovers' fingers down

my thick body, and my leaves
have burst into burning.

I want to glow like embers
that are the fire dying,

growing hotter and hotter
until it's gone.

I want my branching
darkness exposed

by the wind's
transparent insistence

as it pulls, piece by piece,
my bright raiment off.

I want to feel what's next
curled tight as fists inside me.

Lynne Thompson

A BIRTH MOTHER WEARS A COSTUME HER DAUGHTER WILL NEVER FIT IN

Some thought the mother said *taproot*
Some thought that woman said *resigned*

but her daughter mouthed *immaculately conceived*

Some thought the mother said *perdition*
Some thought she said *hocus pocus*

while her daughter wrote parables   wrote charms

Some hoped the daughter would say *yes, honey*
(although they suspected the daughter said *wishbone*—

knew she would deny everything, slipping into, out of)

Some never understood the daughter's need
to be alone, her fear of sorcery—they only knew

her as braid of ginger & sea salt
as weightless darling & origami

Some have heard her bark & bark & bark
Some have heard her arrange a resistance

Lynne Thompson

SOMETIMES, THE LIGHT

—*Joni Mitchell's Ode*

Blue, here is a shell for you,
and sometimes, there will be sorrow
but I have no regrets, Coyote.

We're captive on this carousel of time,
oh, but sometimes   *the light.*
Blue, here is a shell for you and

varnished weeds in window jars.
Why did you pick me and
do you have any regrets, Coyote?

Buy your dreams a dollar down.
Heed the trumpets' call all night.
Blue, here is a shell for you because

the more I'm with you, pretty baby,
I'm like a black crow, flying,
dark and ragged and no regrets.

Until love sucks me back that way,
dreams…dreams and false alarms
but Blue, I've got a shell for you.
What point regrets, Coyote?

Amanda Moore

MORNING HAIBUN WITH TWEEN

The girl can sleep now, hours and hours at a time…years since
the last 2 a.m. tiptoe down the hall to fold herself between us
like a warm sheet. She sleeps now until noon if undisturbed,
later even, forgoing the waking world while her body in sleep
is making a woman. School days she sets an alarm, but it can't
break the caul of her slumber—I crack the door, peel back the
covers, count the minutes: *It's almost 7* I call, careful. Whether
delay tactic or that her teen self has fallen away, she is cuddles
and sweetness, grasping for me, *I love you, Mama* in her soft
low voice. *Five more minutes, please.* Sometimes I can't help it—I
climb in the bed, look at the unguarded face, so ancient and
dear and dangerous: it is like looking at fire. And her hair,
the feel of it as I brush, push it back from the sweet sleeping
countenance I have watched her whole life. When her eyes
flutter open, it is to scowl at me, but when she rides again
toward the crest of sleep, she burrows toward me: her first
comfort. For a moment, I think to change her name to
Sunshine, to Apple Blossom, to Beautiful Repose. But then she
wakens, sour.

Liminality.
I am disoriented
by the constant cross and return.

The girl emerges from the bathroom wrapped in my new
towel. *Hey, that one's mine* I say surprised but not reproachful.
Oh, I thought yours was the tan one, she says, holding the towel
up tight against her new curves. She laughs a little as her
long hair drips onto the hardwood and I catch my breath: this
unfettered version so stunning. *I guess we've both been using*

that one, I say. *Poor tan towel probably thinks we don't love it.* She pauses to decide whether this is funny or offensive and her body coils as if to fling the towel from it. *Eew!* she says, *You used this too?* surprised but not reproachful. She remembers her naked form beneath, snaps the towel shut, scurries to her room, and closes the door firmly. A moment later *Mom* she calls, the door open just one dark sliver and her thin, disembodied arm moving out through the crack, the towel pincered between the pads finger and thumb as if it has turned rancid. *Here* she says as she drops it to the floor. The door closes again.

Shifting intimacies.
We once shared a body but
now not even a towel.

The girl won't make her bus in time and a friend is waiting aboard. She should have to bear the consequences of not waking in time, I think. Still *I'll drive you to the bus stop* I say. She rolls her eyes. *Fine* she says: the new gratitude. She scuffs into her new shoes, flattening down the backs with her heels and then preemptive exasperation with what she thinks will be my protest: *I'll put them on in the car* she says. The digital clock on the dash is reproach. She looks at it and pouts *We'll never make it.* I want my daughter to be hopeful in this life, to persevere, to believe she has agency to do and be…but she's right: we see the bus cross several blocks in front of us and jet up the hill out of sight. Her defeated sigh. *We can catch it* I say, gunning the engine but trying to sound uninvested. *Really?* she says: a glimmer. I turn sharply and speed up the hill and suddenly we are conspiracy, glancing at the end of each block for the bus we want to outrun. I realize I don't know the route: here is the part of her every day I know nothing of, cannot trace. *Go up two more blocks and right* she says, scooting up in her seat, gripping the door, eyes shining. I gun again and swerve. She laughs out loud—it is almost a howl of delight.

Momentary glimpse:
pure childhood joy still lurks beneath
aloofness and cool.

The girl gets out of the car, flips her backpack on one shoulder,
slams the door and bites a quick *Bye* from the air. It is her back
to me again. It is always the back of her I behold, can hold the
longest, have the most time to ponder. We have come through
the morning as if through clear water: I am drenched by it,
but once dry it will leave no mark. The bus kneels to her and
she mounts it as on any other day, happy to greet the driver
who was wondering where she was. Lights flash, slow growl
of engine gathering momentum, my car in gear for the U-turn
that will take me back down to where we started. And then
suddenly her face through the marked glass of the thick bus
window, smiling and waving.

Goodbye, see you, so long
each time more permanent.
So I practice.

NELLE

Jennifer Habel

THE DEATH OF MADAME MONET

1. (May)

She is nearly
always

ill. He is
en plein air.

He cannot lose
the hour.

People wait.
The sun

does not. It's terrible,
he says,

how the light
runs out.

2. (September 5)

In death (as in life)
she decomposes

into color—blue, gray, yellow—
into proportions

of shade
and light. It's his own

fault, he says. He wants
to grasp

the intangible. She was
everything

except there.

3. (September 26)

I am very much
to pity,

because I am
very much

to pity, he writes
his friend.

4. (December)

His coldest
winter. A frozen

river. He wears
three coats

to paint
ice and light.

NELLE

Ice and light,
a white canvas—

his subject,
he'll learn,

is unimportant.

3

Jennifer Habel

THE HABIT OF SAINT THÉRÈSE

She would wish to dream of Him
were she permitted to wish.
Why should she dream of children?
Of butterflies, or birds?
Is she naked under her habit?
Has her nakedness ceased to exist?
Has naked come to mean
gloriously undivided? She is never
lonely now her mind is His. Why
should she dream of children
or butterflies.

15

Erin Adair-Hodges

CLEO

We'd go to Juarez to dance, black light cooing my skin electric
as if invented to love me. All my old selves mewled
in their corner cribs, nursed on dust, unready for the dawn
of such bright. I gave myself a new name, tongued it

into strangers' mouths so they'd know the right me
to miss. I lioned. Ate what my day self feared.
I was Cleo and I was not afraid of karaoke.
Cleo, no blue-mouthed virgin certain

she could worry her way into heaven.
Cleo in a leotard speaking Spanish in an Irish accent, Cleo queering
in that word's pre-verb, Cleo the gypsum dunes
and the bomb they swallow up. Funny—

I am her mother now, though I sometimes
still get her mail. I've curfewed her
but my body's made of windows, lost boys pawing
at the seams. I drink my tea and sleep so hard

it's impossible to know what she's done,
what pleasures she'll bring home to hang on my bones.
I don't know what is a memory
and what is me wanting something dark into life.

Diamond Forde

Black Girl Goes on Vacation to Orange Beach

"[our forefathers and foremothers] too believed that the sea was
the beginning and end of all things, the road to freedom and the
entrance to Guinin,"

—Edwidge Danticat

On the beachside, beer bottles glitter like tombstones
in the sand, a man roots his thumb into coastline
whiter than a waking dream—the ocean yawns. I peer
into her long, jade throat. The man finds a sand flea,
holds it for me to see its shell: bullet-round and
ivory as teeth. He chucks it in his bucket,
mausoleum for the dead he's already caught.
A surfboard spanks the ocean's thigh. She lows with joy.
She has seen enough of death to barely flutter
her lashes, while somewhere beneath her lacy skirts
a legacy of lost bones: waving phalanges,
femurs rooted as trees, sternums clasped on the beat
of the ocean's mothering heart. Sand fleas are not
fleas, instead, crabs spit into the wet band of sand
near the shore to return later by the mercy
of a cold, silver hook. Casket and cradle,
the ocean crosses her legs and waits. We come back
in time. The man claps his hand around another
crab. Without looking the distance has grown between
us, so much, he seems a specter rubied with sun.
I step into the water, the ocean kisses
my calves, my knees, cradles my brown, familiar feet,
then lifts the whole beach out from beneath me, as if
she might carry me everywhere, anywhere I ask, even home.

Susan Taylor Chehak

JANE DOE

Nobody wants to read a story about Iowa, or so I've been told. Nothing happens there, or if something does happen there, it probably isn't anything very interesting, not even to the people to whom it happens, because, on the whole, they're not very interesting either. Even if the story isn't about Iowa per se but is about something that just happened to finally have happened there, nobody would want to read it. Everybody knows that this is true, and no one will blame you if you happen to be somebody who is one of those nobodies yourself.

Most people don't even know where Iowa is, exactly. They have a vague idea, maybe, but they've never been there themselves, and they get it confused with other places all the time, places like Idaho and Illinois and even Ohio, places with *o*'s and *i*'s and maybe an *a*, and what else is there to say? There is nothing special about Iowa. You couldn't write a story about it that would tell anybody anything they don't already know.

Iowa is nowhere and it's nothing. It has no mountains, no sea, no unusual rivers, no great lakes. No big cities, either. It's not even all that flat, not like Nebraska. Or Kansas. It has a lot of fields. And farms, too. But so what? Who doesn't have fields and farms? There are fields and farms everywhere, even in Africa. Even in France. Corn and hogs. Soybeans. Silos and barns and, okay, maybe sometimes the ones in Iowa are pretty, but mostly they're not; mostly they're just what they are, they are what they're for, and they're nothing more or less than that.

Sometimes they stink, but not always. For example, in winter nothing smells like anything at all. It's just cold, and in Iowa it's cold for no good reason that anybody can tell. There's no purpose to the cold or the snow, and it isn't even pretty, mostly. It just is what it is, cold and snow. Lots of cold and lots of snow, but still not as much as plenty of other places get. There is rain, and that's good news for the farmers if there's enough of it, which usually there isn't, or if there isn't too much of it, which usually there is. There are storms, even tornadoes sometimes, but plenty of other places have those, too. The ones they get in Iowa aren't famous or special. For example, the storms that hit Iowa don't have names.

There are woods, too, but not many of them, and they aren't forests—they're neither thick nor deep. They're just woods made up of ordinary trees—oaks and maples and elms, sometimes beeches, a willow here and there; that's all. They cling to the rivers and the streams in the creases of the land.

The animals in Iowa aren't anything you can't find someplace else, either. Pigs, mostly, and cows and horses, donkeys, chickens, goats, sheep. All the usual farm animals, which are maybe interesting at first, when you're a kid, but not for long even then. All the usual wildlife, too: squirrels and skunks, raccoons, turkeys, deer, hawks, owls. You don't see tigers in Iowa. Not even wolves. Or bears.

Except for the hump in its side that is the Mississippi River passing by on its way to and from someplace else, Iowa is just a rectangle in the center of the country, in the center that is not the center at all, but just the middle of the middle, a bit of nothing where nothing interesting happens, where there's nothing interesting to see and not much that's especially interesting to do.

It never happens that something happens in Iowa that hasn't already happened someplace else. It also never happens that something happens in Iowa while nothing else happens in the world, but it does often happen that nothing happens in Iowa when something else happens in the world.

This turns out to be exactly why some people choose to live in Iowa in the first place. Those people like it that nothing happens here, because they don't want anything to happen, at least not to them. They know that sometimes,

when something happens, it's good and it's interesting—or
at least they think that maybe this was once true, at least for
them or for other people that they knew—but that was before
everything that happens started happening to be something
bad more often than it was anything good. Now they know
that, most of the time, when something happens, it's bad; and
although it may still be interesting, it's interesting in a bad way,
and most people don't want bad things to happen, especially
not to them. They've seen bad, they've seen how bad bad
can be, and they don't want those bad things they've seen to
happen to them or to anybody else, either—unless somebody
deserves it, or unless they've asked for it, which some people
do—and so they'd rather be someplace where nothing happens
at all, just to be on the safe side.

By this reasoning, you might think that Iowa is a good
place to raise children, because nothing can happen to a child
here, and that's what good parents want, isn't it? For nothing
to happen to their children? They pray for this, some of them.
Dear God, they say, *please don't let anything happen to* ____. Go
ahead and fill in that blank with the name of your own child,
and you'll see what I mean. Or you can insert your own name
there, and then maybe you'll know something about what it's
like to be a child in Iowa, growing up where nothing happens.
And then you'll also know why some children have to decide
to make something happen when it looks like nothing is ever
going to happen on its own if they don't.

This is called acting out when it gets the child in trouble,
but the parents of the child want to be told that it's really
nothing, that whatever it was that got the child in trouble, still
it's nothing, and so nothing has really happened; everything
is still the same, and it's all okay. They'll agree that the child
was only acting out, and it's over, whatever it was, so now
everybody can just go back to doing nothing and being nothing
again.

It's like a kernel of popcorn—which is a crop that's grown
in Iowa, along with feed corn and seed corn and sweet corn.

Like this: A kernel of popcorn just sits there in the oil until it gets hot enough, and then it starts to swell until it's bigger than its own skin, so it pops, and then it's over, it's nothing. Just air. Even that big event is like nothing happened: there's just the sound of it, that's all, an empty sound, the eponymous pop; and so what if along the way the kernel itself is deformed? That doesn't do anything to anybody except to make them want to eat it. Before it acted out, that kernel was all one thing, perfect and complete, smooth and round and hard; you'd break a tooth if you tried to bite into it. Then *Pop!* just like that, it's soft and deformed and lumpy; and that's what happens to you if you are a girl, and you find yourself in hot oil, and you get popped. At that point you can't help it anymore. You just have to act out. That's a must, and you have no choice. And once that happens—and definitely it will—then that's it, you're done. Finito. One pop, that's all it takes, and after that everything will be changed; and yet nothing will have changed, because you're still there, where nothing happens, and nothing has happened, and nothing is going to happen, because that's how it is; that's how they like it. They want it that way. That is how the place was made.

You already know what they're like, the people who live in Iowa. I don't have to tell you; it's nothing new. They're mostly fat and white and loud and cheerful, and sometimes they're sunburned, or they wear big shorts, or their otherwise straight hair is permed in a tight curly way that is distinctly Iowan. You recognize them because you see them this way when they come to visit you, wherever it is you yourself live. To them, you are an attraction. They are eager and agog, like they've never seen anything like you before; they've never seen the things you see every day and take for granted, except maybe on television or in the movies, where it's either smaller than life or larger than life, but it isn't life, at least not life as they know it, which is just fine with them. And they're friendly, too, and polite. They're all smiles, partly because they want you to like them—because they think that if you like them then probably nothing will happen—but also because they're used to nothing happening and you aren't, and so they feel sorry for you, the way that people who go to the zoo feel sorry for the animals in the cages, because the animals in the cages are stuck there, and they can't go home because they're already home, and it's a terrible home, where all kinds of terrible things can happen and do happen, but these folks from Iowa are free to leave, and they'll go home eventually, home to where nothing happens, while you'll just have to stay right there, wherever you are, and be the ones to whom things happen, both good and bad, but mostly bad.

The people from Iowa pity you for that. They'd like to feed you through the bars. They'd like to baby talk you into feeling happy, if they could, which you know and they know they can't. So, all the time, what they're really hoping for is that you'll jump up and down or beat your chest or do something else that shows them how miserable and trapped you've been feeling, how much you wish that you could be like them, because it makes them happy to know that they have something you don't have, which is nothing. They've read about you in the news, and they've watched you on TV, and they're glad that they're not you, but at the same time they're feeling sorry for you because you are you, and you are not them, and they would never want to be you; but what they don't know is that you would never want to be them, either, because even if you are an animal in a zoo, still at least you're a tiger or a bear or something interesting and dangerous, which is exactly what they are not, and they think they're lucky for that.

Even on those rare occasions when something does happen in Iowa, it's not something that hasn't already happened someplace else, so no matter what happens, somebody somewhere will know what to do to make it seem as if it never happened. That is, whatever happens, it's nothing new in the sense that it's nothing unexpected, which is exactly why some people, certain people, want to go to Iowa to live, with their children, and then that turns out to be why they want to stay there even after their children have grown up and moved away. In fact, these are the people who will want to stay there for the whole rest of their lives. Which they expect to be long, because they think there is nothing that will happen to them there that might make them short. And it's also why certain other people will do anything to get away, as soon as possible. And then, once those people are away, they don't come back; or if they do come back, that's only because something happened while they were away, and it scared them, maybe, or it hurt them, or maybe it was just something that happened that reminded them of what it was like for them when nothing did happen, and they decided they liked that better. This is how it is for people when the something that happens when they weren't in Iowa is something bad.

And then, even when something does finally happen in Iowa, nothing happens.

Like this: In Iowa, when somebody dies, it turns out nothing happened. Even if somebody you thought you loved got hurt. Or if somebody you thought you loved died. Or if somebody you thought you loved almost died, and it was almost all your fault.

For example, let's say there's a girl passed out in the back seat of your car. She's a couple of years older than you, and so you've been led to believe she knows what she's doing. Oh yes, and she's beautiful, by the way. She came into your life like a surprise. You never expected a girl like her to pay any attention to a girl like you, to pick you out of the crowd and smile. Her bright eyes. Her clear face. The way she looked at you, and you could feel the shiver of her radiance on your skin.

Let's say she's passed out in the back seat of your car, like a sleeping princess. You watch the way the leafy trees cast shadows on her body and her face. This is Iowa in summer, so the heat and the humidity are mixing it up into misery. You turn on the car so the air conditioning will blow, but your father has been complaining about how gas prices have lately been going through the roof, so you turn it off again.

This girl told you when you picked her up that her life has not been easy. That she's been on her own for a while now, and maybe she's been living on the street. Her father is a drunk, her mother isn't well, her brothers are cruel, and her grandmother died. You want to be a good person. You want her to be happy. So you helped her get what she said she needed for that. You know that eventually the sun is going to set, and the air is going to cool, and the drugs are going to wear off, and she's going to come to, and she's going to be okay. Maybe she'll reach for you then. Maybe she'll be grateful to you for taking care of her as you have.

You're sitting in the yard of a house that isn't yours, with some friends who aren't really your friends who live there together now that school is out. You still live at home. You ask, "What should we do?" Everyone agrees that it's best to just let her be, let her sleep it off. This sounds reasonable to you.

But then it's getting to be the end of the day, and she's still out there. You check on her again. The fine sweat on her pale skin makes it look like it's not real. Like she might be made of glass. Or porcelain. Like the fine china in your grandmother's dining room that only comes out for holidays when the whole family is there. You watch a bead of sweat gather and then drip, sliding down her jaw, into the shadows of her throat. The tattoo on her shoulder. The bruises on her arms. The blue vein at her wrist. Her slack lips, a wink of tooth. Her eyelashes, caked and smeared in black. She seems so peaceful in her dreams, there inside her own secret self, a million miles away, in a life of unreality where people are walking around, and maybe you'd like to believe you're in there somewhere too.

A car rounds the corner, and you turn to stare at the woman in the front seat, how she's got her hair all done up, and she's passing by here in this world, while in the world behind the girl's eyes, something else is happening. Maybe it's that same woman in the car doing something else altogether, or maybe it's some other woman in some other car, driving slowly past, staring back at you. And you blink, and then the woman and the car are both gone.

That's when you decide you'll have a beer. Just one. You don't really even think about it. It's automatic. There's nobody to keep you from doing anything you want to here. You're not planning on getting wasted, although that's exactly what you'll do. You're just being in the moment, right now, right here, and so you go up onto the porch, where these two guys you don't really know are sitting at the table, playing cards. They offer you a hit, and you take it, and then you get a beer from the cooler and snap it open and light a cigarette and climb into the hammock in the yard. You're listening to the music that comes from a radio somewhere, or maybe it's just in your head. You finish that one beer, and then you get up and get another one. Take two, to save yourself another trip to the cooler. It's been a long time, and you haven't eaten anything for as long as you can remember, so when you roll out of the hammock again, you know you're drunk and *Fuck! That wasn't it. Not to get drunk!* The wobbliness, the blurriness, the fogginess, everything is slowed and sludgy now, and you only wanted to be sharp and clear again. You wanted it to be morning again; the night and its darkness has always seemed too secretive and dangerous to you. And *Fuck!* Now you remember the girl. Those two on the porch have stopped playing cards and are on the chaise making out, and they have no awareness of you or anyone other than themselves.

You go to your car, and there's this sound. At first you think it's the radio, turned down, someone talking in a low voice, saying the same thing over and over again, or repeating a series of numbers. Then it sounds more like a motor, starting and stopping. You open the door, and it gets louder. You put out a hand for balance, and this feels like a dream now because, *What is that sound?* A bellows—whoo-ha, whoo-ha, whoo-ha. And then, in the back seat, there she is. Her eyes are open, and the sound is coming from her, or behind her, or under her. Her chest rises and falls, her eyes roll, so she's not seeing you or anything else at all.

Now you're shaking her, trying to wake her up. "Girl!" you cry. "Girl!" Then it's all loud and happening fast. Those other two are there, because you were screaming, and they see what's happening, so now there's a lot of shouting, some of it your own: "Get her to the hospital! Call 911!"

But those two are pushing you away. They're yelling back at you: "Fuck, no. No ambulance here, man. No cops. Just take her there yourself."

So that's how it ends up belonging to you. All of it. All yours.

By the time you get to the hospital, she's quiet at least. You pull up to the emergency entrance and go inside, and you don't know how you look or what you're saying, but everyone is gaping at you anyway. Like the nurse, or whatever she is, who thinks you're there for yourself, but you're doing your best to explain: "No! She's in the car, a girl, she's...She needs...Help her...Please..." Until finally you get the nurse to follow you outside. And then there's a stretcher, and you say you're just going to park the car, you'll be right back; but instead you drive away, and it's not until you get back home that you realize you never did tell them her name. Maybe you never even knew it yourself.

This is another reason why nothing ever happens in Iowa—because even when it happens, it didn't happen.

You don't have to be a genius or even someone special to know that what I'm saying here is true. You could be anybody, or you could be somebody, or you could be nobody. Or maybe your name's Jane Doe.

Jess Smith

INTERNALIZED

Elizabeth Wurtzel once tried
to soothe me, said it was good to live

the forever bachelorette life.
Why wouldn't I believe her? Maybe

it was the drop of blood
on her fur coat or the fact

of her fur coat at all, or maybe
the speckled chestnut roots spilling

like sludge into her blonde hair.
What's that phrase they say? *It me.*

I wonder if one day I'll be a woman
interviewers ask only about a man

I fucked for a few years
years ago. Maybe fewer

than a few years. But who
can help it? I still love

his name in the room.
Who can help?

I don't eat meat and I would *never*
wear fur. The windows here

are thumb-smudged and struck
with Valentine's glitter. Don't act

as if you've never heard a ghost
wailing from the cellar

and simply turned the sitcom
volume up—Monica Geller's

tirade on tidiness
an aria against remembrance.

Alison Pelegrin

HEIFER

No debutante, no sweet sixteen, in prom pics
freaky tall, exiled by the cheerleaders
from their pyramid but on-call as anchor
in a tug-of-war, bone crusher, hurler of javelins
at Sister Ambrose across the field. In yoga,
where we are all one, I am more like one and a half,
a starved down XXL unable to swap clothes
with anyone I know. Frumpy, hugely maternal,
an elephant streaming tears as I move logs,
except I've grown to like the work of slinging weight.
Now, at the gym, having learned to strut my size,
I will settle on a bro to nitpick and outlift,
kilo plates rattling on the bar as I uproot it in a flash.
In high school, the nuns taught us that our thumbs
could poke out perverts' eyes. Protecting
our maidenhood, they made it seem like a sport,
and I couldn't wait to make the team, virginal
in the extreme, violently devoted and pure,
like the fantasy girl they praised, who dropped
to all fours, chewed grass, and mooed,
shitting her pants to stave off dishonor.
I got my chance to lash out against a man,
the cop who confiscated my fake ID
and drove me home, one hand on the wheel
and one under my shirt. I thought it was punishment
for my lies and amaretto buzz, so I held still,
and didn't claw his eyes out or bellow or screech.
He said I was lucky to get off with a warning,
and, recalling virgin martyr Saint Maria Goretti
and her 14 stab wounds, I suppose he was right.

Leigh Anne Couch

Life is a State of Siege,
a War to the Last Woman

—Randall Jarrell

Of all the gin joints in all the towns in all the world, I walk into his
           and right back out again to call my family: It's going to be awhile.

I need this drink with this man from two lives and three towns back,
           where spoons and forks tangled the yards.

His hands on my body I don't need but I might have hidden parts
           of myself in his, so let me flesh out my past

on those Revolutionary War streets where I rented rooms for nothing
           in an old boardinghouse, becoming the only tenant and caretaker

of rabbits and yellowjackets simmering in groundnests. I need this man,
           who is not my husband, to break in my heart its love of endings,

its longing for the dying engines of twilight when the dishes are clean,
           the laundry folded, the boys asleep. Not only childhoods get misla

in the terror of afternoons strangled into meaninglessness.
           What would that girl who ate bread and cheese under a bridge

on a dirty beach with strangers want with my life? How I miss her and
           the letter writer, lizard of many, dance-hall girl, lugger of sandsto

stacker of wood, thrift queen, bookstore haunt, tinkerer of spaces—
           my dear companions dwindled to one, siloed and happy—

ther-wife. I'll be home soon. For now I long to be fluid, a tributary
          for all those selves rushing and laughing into our home. I know you all

uld love me. This old boyfriend with eager eyes writes his number on a napkin
          and I take it. I take it to mean it's time to pack up, return

se rooms to vacancy, strip the sheets, bank the fire, turn the knob quietly
          on my own sleeping house, and climb into bed with my youngest,

lank with the warm damp smell of him. His words, thick and dreamclogged,
          have you had enough of me, momma? burst my heart like a ripe fig.

Lana K. W. Austin

Origin Story: Flying Lessons

The bird hallelujahs itself up
above the nature preserve
across from my house, and I believe
I can hear each wing push against
not just air but something more
like joy, and the trees, as if finally
setting their desire free like when
I said you absolutely must spend
more time on my nipples, quiver
expectantly beneath all this
commotion, even in winter
with the bones of the things
licked clean or in summer when
every leaf shimmies in time
to the constant throng above
with the hawks, herons, and even
simple robins knowing they are
part of a living mystery, the sky,
which is both home and not home
to everything that takes flight,
which includes me, since I'm
awake now, intensely alive as I
lift off from the ground, all of me
leaping wildly into the new.

Jessica Turney

TONIC IMMOBILITY

I hear *hey girl, get in* and my grip tightens
around the gas pump. I stop the tap of my foot,
wince each time the Valero sign flickers, its neon
lights frantic, showering me with shards
of light, only for a second, gone, then back.
I look up and see a car, shadows of men
in the front seat, in the back and *didn't you hear
me bitch, I said get in* and of course I hear him,
but my voice takes flight, leaves my body.
I try to say something, try to make out more
than just shadows. I think of that time

my sister and I came across a dying seal,
its body spilling onto the stone steps
leading up to our hotel; my sister ran
for help, wind in her lungs, carrying
her far from me; I just stood there, scared,
watching it breathe; each breath distanced
itself from the next. I couldn't cry or wrap
my body around the beast, couldn't avoid its eyes,
black suns, face pointed toward sky—

there are six eyes staring at me from the shadows
of the car, waiting for me to get in so they can drive
me to a place I'll never see, and I can't say *no*
or *yes* or *fuck you* or even call for help,
and my mother isn't here to pull me away
from the dying seal, its eyes almost closed,
face reaching toward light.

Rachel Hall

JILTED

From the doorway of the Dogwood cabin, Lil can see her friends, Janet and Becca, with two boys. They're standing in front of the Snack Shack. Beyond them is the lake, glistening in the afternoon sun, and on its far side are the boys' cabins named after Indian tribes. One of the boys is tall and thin; the other is red-headed and stockier. Her friends keep flipping their long hair, Becca's honey colored and down to her butt, Janet's, dark and glossy, reaching past her shoulders. They're like fillies, her friends—all long legs and long pretty hair, flipping and flicking. A big group of younger campers and their counselor pass in front of Lil, blocking her view briefly. When they've moved on, Lil sees Janet swat at the redheaded boy. He howls, grabs his arm as if mortally wounded. They all laugh harder. Becca bends at the waist, laughing, taking the opportunity to flip all her hair over, a curtain of gold, and then back. When she stands, she moves behind the tall boy, places her hands on his shoulders, and hops on his back for a piggyback ride. This is stunning to Lil. How have they learned to do this? It's a betrayal. Janet and Becca were supposed to be waiting for her by the cabin door while she applied calamine lotion. She's already on this first day at Camp Silver Lake been bitten up. It had taken only a second to dab herself with calamine, but when she got to the door, they were gone. Glancing at her leg now, she sees the calamine has dripped down in gloppy, pink rivulets.

The plan had been to get slushies at the Snack Shack before afternoon activities. It's hot at Camp Silver Lake, the air August thick, pressing down on her. Lil wants a slushy, but it seems impossible to join her friends as long as those boys are there. In the last few months, around the time she turned twelve, she's been hit hard by virulent strain of self-consciousness. Before, she'd been a leader, the one gathering up teams, telling everyone where to go; she was outspoken, loud even, not carefree but happy and energetic. Full of ideas and plans. Now, though, everything is awkward, painful. People might look at her, might see or hear or detect—what? What must she hide? Everything, but that's not entirely true. A part of her wants to be noticed, too. Noticed and admired.

She wishes her hair were straight and long, worthy of admiration. Instead, it curls and frizzes and is controlled only by yanking it back into a ponytail or a braid. She makes herself walk towards her friends, past the showers and the path for the mess hall. The gravel crunches loudly beneath her tennis shoes, announcing her entrance. "Hi," she says when she gets to the Snack Shack patio. She comes to a stop behind Janet, hoping she'll step back, open the circle to her.

"Oh, hi," Janet says, turning her sleek, dark head slightly.

"Hi," says Becca.

Neither of them are rude, she can't say that, but neither are they welcoming. "I thought you were waiting for me," she says, hating how she sounds—grasping, babyish. Becca might say so, except the boys have all her attention. They are punching at each other, hooting with each jab. It's horrible standing there, just outside the circle. Mortifying. She wants to disappear.

"What's so funny?" Becca demands of the boys. "Tell us!"

The whistle blows then—three short blasts—indicating the end to free period.

"Can't, gotta go!" says the tall boy. Both boys race off, gravel crunching under their tennis shoes. Maybe her friends will be their old selves, nicer now with the boys gone, but they glide off to archery, without another word to her. Maybe she has disappeared. She can hear them giggling together as they head up the hill.

Somehow, though they all signed up for the same activities and order of preference, Becca and Janet have the same schedule, and Lil is alone with new kids except for Brenda Buckholtz. She's not friends with Brenda, but they're in the same grade at school. Brenda is a giant with a big, booming voice. And, now at swimming, she comes right over to Lil. She has greasy streaks of sunscreen on her arms and face.

"Hi," she says. She stands before Lil like a little kid, pigeon-toed, her belly sticking out under her dumb one-piece suit.

"Hi," Lil says, glancing away. Today is testing to see what groups they're in. Lil is a good swimmer, so she's confident she won't have to worry about Brenda after today. She imagines Brenda's big bones will pull her down like a hulking vessel, a shipwreck of a girl.

Tammy, the swimming counselor, is deeply tanned and has zinc oxide on her tiny, snubbed nose. She wears mirrored sunglasses, so it's hard to see where she's looking. "You," she points to Brenda and five others, "go ahead out to the raft, circle it, and return using standard crawl."

One girl whimpers about the water temperature as she wades in.

"Quickly," Tammy says. "Let's go!"

Lil is surprised to see that Brenda is a good swimmer. She's back well before the others.

"Ok," Tammy says, "wait there." The weaker swimmers trail in, and are told to wait in different spots. Another group goes, then another. When it's Lil's turn, she steps into the water. It feels good, cool after the hot midday sun. Lil considers going slowly so she can avoid being put in Brenda's group, but she can't stand to not do her best. She kicks hard, her arms slice the water. She beats the others in her group. When she steps onto the deck, she's breathing hard, but she feels good, like herself for the first time since she's arrived at Camp Silver Lake.

"Nice job," Tammy says. She indicates that Lil should join Brenda's group on the beach.

"Goody!" Brenda says, patting the spot next to her. "Come sit by me," she says.

Tired, Lil complies. There's no shade on the beach, and right away Lil can feel the sun burning her. She doesn't want to talk to Brenda, so she lies back on the beach, sifts the pebbly sand through her fingers. She closes her eyes and sees bright orange through her eyelids.

Swimming is what Lil did with her father before the divorce last year, before he married his graduate student, Lee Ann. It had been their Saturday morning routine from the time she learned to swim. They'd go to the college gym when it opened, leaving her mother in her bathrobe and her little brother Jason watching cartoons and clutching his blanky.

Lil loves the echo-y hush of the pool, the balmy air. She loves, too, the blue of the tiles, the way the waves make the lines wavy beneath her. Back and forth, they went, flipping at the end of each lap, pushing off again. Afterwards, she likes the tingling sensation in her arms and legs, the way the chlorine smell lingers on her skin and hair. On the way to the car, her father might pat her damp head, call her "his little fish." They didn't say much, but there was an easiness between them, something light and effortless. Now, her feelings about her father are muddled by her awareness of her mother's sadness and rancor. When her mother mentions her father, it's always spiteful, barbed. And her father won't come in the house anymore, won't even come to the door when he picks them up for dinner on Wednesday nights. He honks, and Lil and Jason know to go out. You can bet their mother has something to say about this, too.

"Okay, kiddos," Tammy says, stopping at the group comprised of Brenda, Lil, and two others. "I'd like you to consider participating in Swimmerthon at the end of the session."

"What is it?" Brenda asks.

"It's a one-mile swim. We do it here," Tammy says, pointing over her shoulder with her thumb. "If you sign up, we'll have special practices to build endurance during free period. Everyone who finishes the mile gets a certificate. The winner gets a trophy."

"I want to do it," Lil says. She can imagine herself slicing through the water, leaving a bubbly wake. She imagines the trophy on her shelf at home.

"Hold your horses," Tammy says. "Signup is tomorrow at breakfast. We've got to get everyone sorted into the right classes first."

That night in her bunk below Janet, Lil can hear her friends whispering even though the rule is no talking after lights out. When they'd selected bunks that morning, she'd thought sharing one with Janet was a good plan, didn't consider Becca and Janet would be at the same level on top and that they'd team up and leave her out. They weren't even that good of friends—it was she, Lil, who had brought them together, who told them about Camp Silver Lake. The camp is famous for its horse trails that run beside the Current River and up along the gray bluffs. Every camper gets one early morning ride per session. You don't know when it's your turn until a red bandana is tied to your bunk. Lil can't wait for her turn; she's imagined this for months—galloping through a field of wildflowers, her hair flying behind her, her horse leaping over bushes and fast-moving streams. In her fantasy, there are no counselors or other campers, just her and her friends, the sun rising pink and golden before them.

She can't make out what Becca and Janet are saying even if she hangs her head over the side and concentrates. "What are you talking about?" she whispers, but there is no response. "Hey," she says, louder.

From her post by the door, Melanie says, "No talking, Lil!"

It's not fair. She's not the only one talking. Lil's bug bites itch and sting; the bunk's sheets feel rough, scratchy against her sunburn. She pokes the bottom of Janet's bunk with her toes, once, then twice. She can feel Janet shift above. She pokes again, harder this time.

"Stoppit, Lil!" Janet hisses.

Lil lies very still so the stiff sheets and Janet's sharp words won't smart. In the morning, maybe she'll tell Melanie she's not feeling well and ask to call her mother. She can say she's changed her mind, she doesn't want to go to sleepaway camp, after all.

After a while, the only noises in the cabin are the snuffles of sleep and the bunk springs creaking as someone turns. Melanie makes the rounds, checking that everyone is asleep. Lil pulls the covers over her head as Melanie comes down their row. She doesn't want to be noticed or consoled. Once Melanie has passed, Lil pulls the covers back down. From her bunk, she can see Melanie slip out the door. In a moment, she smells cigarette smoke. Then, after another moment, she hears Melanie's voice and a male voice joining hers, both of them receding.

Why does she tell them? She's not fully awake when she reports that she saw Melanie leave. Janet has been French braiding Becca's hair on Lil's lower bunk, but she stops, lets Becca's thick blond braid unravel. She looks hard at Lil. "She leaves?"

"Yeah, when she thinks we're all asleep. She meets some guy, I think."

"Maybe it's Tripp," Becca says. "He's super cute."

"That's not the point," Janet says. "Don't you get it?"

"What?" Lil says, but she can guess.

"Never mind," Janet says and resumes her braiding.

The campers are required to write two letters home each week. Lil writes one to her mother and one to her father. To her mother, she writes about Becca and Janet's defection. To her father, she writes about the Swimmerthon and the endurance practices, how they will work up from a quarter-mile to a half-mile by the end of the first week.

Over the next few days, Lil makes friends with a girl

from arts and crafts—Robin. Like her, Robin is doing the Swimmerthon, and she loves horses, so they spend all their free time swimming or in the stables with its gambrel roof and dirt floor, the whole place thick with the sweetish smell of hay and manure. It's all girls there, even Annie, the riding teacher, who's older than the counselors. She might let them brush out the lesson ponies or muck out a stall. Each girl has a favorite horse. For Lil, it's Pixie, a chestnut mare with a long, dark mane. After a couple days, Pixie seems to recognize her, throws her head back in greeting. Robin likes a roan called Betty-Boop. When Lil explains the situation with Janet and Becca to her, Robin nods. "Boy crazy," she says, rolling her eyes. She's the youngest of five girls, so she's seen it before. "It's a bad phase."

Lil smiles. A phase can only last so long. She'll wait it out. She has endurance.

There are only two problems with the swim practices, as Lil sees it, and they have nothing to do with swimming. Brenda Buckholtz is participating, and she tags after Lil and Robin, which wouldn't be so bad if the boy Becca likes—Kevin— hadn't begun coming to practices. His very presence in his red swim trunks makes Lil feel small and sweaty. He ignores her, but surely he knows she's Becca's friend. Or have Janet and Becca pretended they don't really know her, as she tries to do with Brenda?

When Tammy calls roll, Kevin laughs at Brenda's name.

"What's that, Kevin?" Tammy says.

"Nothing," he says, smirking.

When he sees Lil looking at him, he makes an ugly face— his mouth agape, his brows knit—that she knows is meant to mirror hers. She turns away, burning.

"What a jerk," Robin says.

Because swimming makes her tired, she sleeps through Becca and Janet's first nighttime escape. She realizes it only because they're both logy the next morning. When they are finally roused, she sees they've slept in their clothes. Becca has pine needles stuck to her hair. When Janet sees them, she points and bursts into laughter. "Oh my god," she says, "I'm going to pee in my pants!" She bolts from the cabin. Becca tugs the clump of needles from the back of her head. She gives Lil a look that says, *stay quiet*.

Lil thinks her friends are being stupid. She thinks Kevin and Mike are obnoxious. Whenever they see Brenda, for instance, they call her Brenda Butthole. And yet, her friends' exploits flatten her activities, turn them shabby and dull. Even the early morning ride isn't as she'd hoped. The horses are all harnessed together and trod the path by rote. They might as well be going around and around like carnival ponies. There is no galloping, of course, because the group has a range of riders, some with little experience at all. Lil's horse (not Pixie) keeps trying to eat the grass when they slow, and even though it's early, the air is heavy and moist. Lil spends most of the ride looking forward to it ending so she can strip off her jeans, boots, and the long socks, remove the heavy riding helmet. The sun when it rises is muffled by the thick haze.

The grounds at night feel different. Lil can hear sounds in the woods, branches creaking, leaves rustling. During the day these sounds are masked by the chatter and movement of the campers, the whistles that divide the day into periods and sessions. It's very still now, the air thick and heavy. Not long ago, Lil would suggest that there were fairies and sprites who only came out at night living in the trees. She knows better than to mention this to Janet and Becca. And besides, they're too far ahead of her. Lil is feeling pretty smart that she went to bed fully dressed, that she was able to stay awake, and that when Janet and Becca made their move, she simply followed them. They couldn't tell her not to without risking waking someone.

Once they are out of the cabin and into the woods, Janet

turns and demands to know what she thinks she's doing.

"What's it look like?" Lil says.

Janet and Becca walk ahead of her, annoyed. They don't hold back the low branches, so Lil has to duck or stay back to avoid getting thwacked in the face. She follows them to the clearing where Sunday services are held. There's a stage with a podium up front and big logs with notches cut out of them for seats.

What has she imagined? A large group of kids? A guitar and a bonfire? Maybe she thought they'd skinny dip? She hasn't really thought this through, but she's disappointed when she sees that it's only Kevin and Mike. The boys are lying back on the logs.

"Boo!" Becca says, coming up behind Mike.

"Haha," he says. "I'm so scared." And then seeing Lil, he adds, "What's she doing here?"

"Hey, it's Butthole's friend," Kevin says.

"No, I'm not!" Lil says.

"No, I'm not!" Kevin repeats.

"She made us," Janet says. "Sorry." She's moved to Kevin's side and is draping herself over him.

"It's a bit tight here," Mike says. "If you know what I mean." He leads Becca off.

Lil can hear their footsteps trailing off. Janet and Kevin have disappeared, too, or at least she can't see them. She's feeling decidedly less smart now, like she might cry. She's afraid to walk back alone, afraid to sit here, too. Carefully, feeling her way from log to log, she makes her way to the stage. Here, she can lie down, she figures. Wait. She thinks of her mother at the door when she and Jason come back from visiting their father, the thin line of her lips. Lil claws at her mosquito bites, even though the scratching makes them itch more, bleed, and sting.

The worst thing is the way they've talked about her as if she weren't there. Their scorn—or is it disregard?—gets folded into who she is, how she sees herself: unwanted. She's too young, too self-absorbed to understand this has nothing to do with her. Nothing at all. But how can it feel otherwise?

Lil will forget much of this summer. She'll forget about the horror of being thrown together with Brenda Buckholtz, the predictable name the boys called her. She'll forget about Pixie's soft mouth eating from her palm. She'll forget the words to the camp song and the ghost stories, even the one about the Beauty of the Bluffs whose sad, sad song about the brave who spurned her can be heard on certain windy days. Even after she has boyfriends, lovers, one husband, then another, what remains from that summer is the jilting—the suddenness of her friends' disinterest and abandonment, the surprise and smack of it. The time before boys—she will long for it all her life.

The next thing she knows, she's being nudged awake. A flashlight shines into her face, so she can't see who it is.

"What do we have here?" Melanie says. She's with the Redbud counselor, Jennifer. Behind them are Becca and Mike, Janet and Kevin. Janet's shirt is on inside out.

"I don't know," Lil says, shielding her eyes from the flashlight.

"She got left at the altar," Jennifer says, gesturing to the podium, laughing.

"Alright, let's go, all of you," Melanie says over their laughter. "You, too, Miss Havisham."

Punishment is doled out equally—dishwashing and kitchen clean-up—but Lil is the only one ridiculed. It's as if the others have participated in a normal camp caper, while she's some weirdo tag-a-long. Becca and Janet make no pretense of friendship after that night. It's not her fault they got caught, she wants to say. She didn't do anything, but they won't even talk to her as they wipe down the tables in the mess hall. The cloying smell of bleach and wet rag will linger on her hands all day.

Thank goodness for the Swimmerthon, for the practices which Tammy makes fun with games and races. They are all swimming half a mile or more by now. A few of the youngest kids have bailed, but there's still a strong group of dedicated swimmers, maybe a dozen. Swimming, everything else falls away—stupid Kevin and Mike, her friends' defection, her father's. She's not a girl anymore, not Miss Havisham, but a fish, the water silky and cool, her mind on movement. Underwater, she can see only green.

In the final days of their session, the rain that's been threatening to come all week arrives. It pings against the roof of the cabin, drips from the eaves. Lil falls asleep to the sound of it, wakes to more. It doesn't cool things down, so it's wet and steamy, and everyone is sticky and cross in their rain ponchos and slickers. Mushrooms grow bulbous and huge in the woods. Thighs stick to the benches and chairs in the mess hall, make an embarrassing smacking sound when they stand. Most activities go on despite the rain, but the endurance practices have twice been canceled because of lightning. The dance, which Lil has been dreading, doesn't get canceled. Instead, it's held in the mess hall rather than on the tennis courts as planned. A real DJ is brought in, and a disco ball spins from the rafters.

The girls in the Dogwood cabin have been planning their outfits all day, swapping clothes to get their look just right. Lil is wearing a striped T-shirt of Robin's and her own cut-offs. Earlier that day, Janet and Becca braided their wet hair into dozens of tiny braids for a crimped effect. Under the disco ball's sparkle, they put on a show, shake their ripply hair, shimmy together, laughing. The little girls from Spruce are all dancing together in a big cluster, singing at the top of their lungs. Lil knows she did that with her friends at sleepovers not even that long ago, but it seems impossible. Now she can think only of how she looks on the dance floor—how others might see her, what they would think. She moves minimally next to

Robin and some others from her cabin. Lil is worried that no one will ask her to dance and that someone will. And then what? She'll have to stand close to some sweaty boy, sweating herself. It's excruciating to imagine.

Then the music changes to something slow; Tripp and Melanie move to the middle of the dance floor, wrap their arms around each other, and sway to "If You Leave Me Now." The lights dim. The room seems to hush with reverence and wonder. Then Kevin and Janet join them. Soon, Mike and Becca are there, too. Mike has his hands low on Becca's back, nearly on her butt. Lil has to look away.

"Let's get popsicles," Robin says.

It's a relief to leave the dance floor, the worshipful awe as the couples dance.

They each eat two grape popsicles, the best flavor, they agree. They show each other their purple tongues then go cross-eyed trying to see their own. They stay outside even after the music turns fast again.

They've had to push back the Swimmerthon because of the rain and thunderstorms, so this morning, the last day of camp, is the last possible time. Lil has imagined an audience standing on shore, a regatta of canoes filled with campers cheering them on, but most kids are still packing up, stuffing smelly, muddy clothes into duffels and trunks, collecting tie-dyes and macramé from arts and crafts, using up the last of their account in the Snack Shack. It's just Tammy and the assistant swim coach, Wendy, on the dock. The swimmers have lost ranks; it's just five of them now. Lil, Robin, Brenda, and two boys from Cherokee. No Kevin.

The sun is out, but meekly, in a provisional sort of way. Tammy goes over the rules and safety precautions again, and then they're off, splashing into the silky green of the lake. Lil knows to pace herself, to save some steam for the end. For a long time, it's easy, and then it gets harder. That's how it always is. She knows this, knows that if she keeps going, it gets easy again. A rhythm develops, clock-like, and she's just arms and legs, heart and lungs, her brain fully focused.

She doesn't notice that Robin has stopped because of cramps. That Brenda is slowing. That the younger boys, who started out fast, are struggling. The sky has turned gray, then bruised and yellowish. Is that a crack of thunder? She hears Tammy and Wendy calling her from the dock, sees them waving their arms. "Lil! Come on back!" Their words come to her in wisps. "Lillian!" She can see the mile marker bobbing in the near distance. The sky is dark and low, a lid coming down. She keeps going.

Charlotte Pence

ALLIGATOR SWIMMING PAST

A green-black nub breaks
the bayou's brackish skin.
A piece of wood to overlook—

until it moves. The back
now rises into being
like a mountain range.

This is the way the world
forms itself: from nothing
to a broiling something

that glides in toothy silence
past my kayak toward
its muddy bank of dented grass

and clicking tips of wild rice
where red-winged blackbirds
dip, and turtles cleat higher on

their log as the gator, like
the rest of us, locks in
on thoughts of what's next.

Michelle McMillan-Holifield

SALT, AS A LOVE LETTER

From the restaurant deck, we view
       the ocean as a globe,
    a velvet world
where round waves of salt-loam
       moving against a mud-slick shore
       sound like soul-heavy cellos:
relentless moans
       of an insomniac longing for dreams.
    You order charbroiled oysters and steamed broccoli.
The waiter praises
       your oyster choice, ticking off a list of non-committal
    foodwords he heard somewhere.
I imagine, instead, salt
          dissolving
       on fluttered sprouts, sluicing between
leafy floret nailtips
          sliding, as nectar, down the stems,
       their soft spines
awash in briny blessing. Green nodes gossiping
       along your palate
       conspiring together. Inspiring. And I long to be the velvet world
you sail to
       and the ocean that gets you there
       where salt,
in all its melodious states, is our savored secret, a love letter
       embroidered
       on the shore of your tongue.

Natasha Deonarain

PRETORIA, SOUTH AFRICA, 1945

The backyard overlooks the neighbor's
cemented clothesline, flat-topped like a
baobab draped in snapping
multi-colored leaves and she's five-years-old—
says my mother six months before
she turns seventy-nine.

She makes the swing from rope taken
from her father's shed, throws two long pieces over
the strongest branch she can find, knots each under the
plank

      and climbs on top, spraying small clouds of red dust
over shiny shoes
as she kicks herself off the ground;

back and forth and higher and higher—

until suddenly
her legs catch on the clothesline
and she's hanging there, brown-gold pigtails
stretching to the concrete below.

She doesn't scream or cry, she says, laughing
on the other end of a long-distance phone call and no one
comes to help but
she's not sure if she's got the story right,

remembering the pain, the scars on the
back of her knees
and if she could turn around she might find them again.

NELLE

I see her free in the segregation of where I was born,
kicking dust,
kicking rooftops and clouds, scars fading from her knees and broken
right hip,
        alone on the floor in the dark
as momentum swings her body
back and forth,
higher and higher, black patent shoes
and white-lace socks kicking, kicking against a clear blue sky.

Abriana Jetté

MAMA ALWAYS WARNED THEY STILL HATE THE JEWS

—after Charlottesville

The doors to the train opened like always
so I walked inside but plastered on the seats
were red swastikas
I had to sit on a swastika
on my way to work and everyone was so
uncomfortable and nobody spoke I stared
blankly at my purse and thought why am I silent
I thought I guess it could be worse
as I sat on a swastika, granddaughter of
Abraham and of Anna, survivors
Auschwitz, Dachau
it was an ordinary day
I know I'm repeating myself when I say
I was in Brooklyn
riding the train to work with red swastikas
it was silent and the air felt heavy with quiet
but not the good kind   really not quiet at all
this quiet was the quiet of being
transported the quiet
my grandmother heard on the trains if you
want to call them that pitch black
babies crying heading who knows where for who knows
how long that's the type of quiet
I stayed quiet on the train with the swastikas
wondering who at the New York City Metropolitan
Transit Authority gave this idea the go ahead
looked over the plans and said why not

figured even better make the swastikas a bold
loud red advertise this on every train you can
someone said yes because   it's no big deal and
we want people to notice   don't let them forget
we're still here   we have always been here
everywhere someone said decorate the train with swastikas
and I hopped on like I had every other day before
stepped inside looked around sat down in silence
with two dozen other people in the same car
we rode the same train same route same
humdrum ride to work
and here we are just a few years later
which one of us will speak first

Jessie LaFrance Dunbar

ON THE BURIAL OF PECOLA BREEDLOVE AND FINDING VOICE THROUGH TONI MORRISON

Six years before I was cut from my mother's womb, a woman named Chloe Anthony Wofford Morrison dreamt of me. She named me Pecola. Pecola Breedlove, though all we seemed to breed was loathing. Unlike the girls with wavy hair and lighter skin, Pecola and I received no notes from crushes with "yes," "no," "maybe" boxes to check from boys with crushes. My teachers shrugged off my cornrows as they taught the girls in health class the proper way to brush their hair, from ends to root, one hundred times per night. They assigned Dick and Jane readers with stay-at-home moms, white picket fences, plenty of food, and white, freckled faces. Meanwhile, I did my homework by candlelight when my single mother couldn't pay Con Edison, then crawled in bed beside her in our one bedroom apartment and dreamt of being not simply present, but gifted…with beauty. But like *The Bluest Eye* had been before me, I was banned from public consumption—a story too ugly to be told.

I was too black to have a story and too female to tell it, let alone to be protected—even in my grandmother's porcelain bathtub—from the manicured hands of the aunt who promised to bleach the black off of me, from the uncles and cousins who choked me to secrecy. I was a victim of the country's original sin, and so were they.

Though I was quite meek, my narrow, dark, female body, adorned in ill-fitting hand-me-downs was a general affront. The marks of blackness, femaleness, and poverty became a canvas for new scars: rocks, fists, molestations, ribbons tied around my neck until my eyes bulged, urine-soaked clothing from being locked in closets for hours, busted lips, and tear tracks that remained like prison tattoos. I could do nothing about the economic circumstances into which I was born, nor did it occur to me that God could help with such a thing. But at least I was not done becoming, though my innocence was gone. If I transformed into a pretty, white swan, I would be safe. Since I had been told that God helps those who help themselves, I started by dedicating myself to the respectability politics into which so many black children are primarily, secondarily, and tertiarily socialized. Don't dress too provocatively. Learn to speak King's English. Get good grades. Go to church. Be seen and not heard. Obey authority and understand that you have none.

The first of many to touch me in unnarratable ways gave me an offering of redemption and coping through the Twenty-Third Psalm, which I was to memorize and repeat like a circus animal before eyes moistened by hundred-proof tears.

The Lord is my shepherd. I shall not want. He maketh me to lie down in green pastures. He leadeth me beside still waters. He restoreth my soul...Yea though I walk through the valley of the shadow of death, I shall fear no evil, for thou art with me. Thy rod and thy staff, they comfort me.

Neither Pecola nor I was comforted by the words, for there was no staff that prevented the transgression of natural boundaries we had suffered. Yet, despite all our commonalities, I recognized divergences between Pecola and me. She wanted blue eyes, which, to me, was ludicrous. Blue eyes in a black face would be startling, unsettling like those black face performers with the stark white eyes and red liver lips. No, hazel, or green, that would endear me to the others. I was also smarter than Pecola: I knew the eyes would make me see the world differently, but to be seen, I also needed lighter (fairer?) skin, longer (straighter?) hair, nostrils that didn't flare when the audacity to smile occasionally struck me, and lips thin enough to be colored with a single pass of gloss. But it was not simply about ugliness or beauty. For me, these devotions were about survival.

In an act of defiance, I got a diary with a lock and key and began to write my own words after Pecola—explaining myself to an audience to whom I did not exist. I reframed myself as powerful instead of pathetic, pretending to be free from the impetus to write to those who, like me, had been colonized—physically and psychologically. I closed myself off to the world, in the protection of my mother's living room, filled with the smell of Marlboro cigarettes and vodka, furniture not yet paid off but in various states of disrepair, and I began to reflect. By age fifteen, I developed an imagination as a form of escapism, and my first image was to conceive of what it might be like to be the:

Teacher's Pet

She is not to be pitied

If anything admired, but never told

Not knowing is half her beauty.

You mustn't blame her for her knees

Darker than can't-see-at-night

Her prayers are long

And the rickety wooden floor is merciless.

You needn't empathize with her

She can barely walk in her own shoes

The soul's worn at the edges.

Just allow her to sit in the back of the classroom

Silently

While other children read fairytales aloud.

Because when the three o'clock bell rings

She'll have her brother and two sisters to pick up from daycare

She'll extend hands that bear the burden of age that her face is

too innocent to know.

She'll stop at a crossroad

And remind the children to wait

Until the tiny white man lights their path.

She'll cross over

And find herself in

The Projects.
If the elevator is running,
The doors will open and markings on the wall
Will shout obscenities at her.
But she takes no offense.
She simply holds her breath
(half because of what may be behind her front door
and half because there is fresh urine on the elevator floor.)
Arriving at 4D
She'll flick the switch.
If the lights come on, she'll cook those last two whitings in
the freezer.
If not, she'll do her homework by candlelight.
Never understood how ten could actually be
Ten years-old.
So, when she sits in the back of the classroom
Listening to fairytales
Let her be.

From my birds-eye view in the back of classrooms, I could see that not everyone had to follow these imperatives. There were bold little Asian girls and Latinas with proximity to whiteness, who voiced their opinions and took their rightful places in the front row[s]—comparatively undeterred in their becoming. But Pecola and I had been systematically dehumanized...invisible to empathy and highly conspicuous to abuse. So, we developed coping strategies that we mistook for our personalities. My discomfort with the gaze meant that I was shy. My silence was accompanied by whispers of "that girl not too bright, is she?" With the little I had to give, I became generous to a fault because affection, or at least the absence of violence, could be purchased with plagiarized homework assignments, collected candies from teachers for good behavior, favorite pencils. I could see them, the friends I coveted, but not that I was beggar with my own riches. I gave it all away just to navigate through each painful second. What I endured was not a childhood. And if you know anything about Toni Morrison, you know that she

believed that far too many black girls were, similarly, deprived.
After all, Beloved—a two-year-old child—walks out of the
water in the body of a nineteen-year-old woman...

Despite horrors that have brought literally all of my
counselors to tears, Toni Morrison taught me that there were
advantages to my perspective from the back of the room. Yes,
I was demonstrably "ugly" and "deserving" of very little, but
there were reasons for it—reasons that had been carved into
wet cement and left to solidify over centuries, well before God
thought the world needed one of me—a Breedlove. Dick and
Jane, the Cleavers and the Bradys, they were symptoms and
reinforcements, but they did not *make* me ugly. Nor did the
white dolls or birthday cards with little white girls flaunting
flower-adorned pigtails. The thing is, when one is imprisoned
and placed in solitary confinement for what Louis Armstrong
would call the sin of black (and blue) skin, deconstruction,
rather than prayer, becomes a saving grace. While I was asking
myself why God would thrust me in this body and allow me
to choke on heaping spoonfuls of poison, Morrison was telling
me how people willfully misread The Word, and that people,
as a collective, were only as good as they treated the least of us.

Who was responsible? It wasn't Pecola, or Me, or Cholly
or Polly, or Eartha or Isadore. I *had* to know who and why
in order to understand who and what I am. My prayers
and abstinence from things human and worldly offered no
reasonable solutions; they had only darkened my knees and
left me restless, so I closed The Good Book, abandoned the
psalms...and opened texts—some of them novels like *The
Bluest Eye*, some of them scholarly, all of them by people who
looked like me. I learned that I was from Africa and that some
genius of psychological warfare had shrunken my continent
on the world map and by extension had shrunken me into
a minority in a world that was overwhelmingly populated
by Me's. I learned that my color had been criminalized and
that the criminal justice system was the progeny of the slave
patrol. I learned that the light skin and straight hair my mother
inherited was the result of centuries of violations, not unlike

the ones that Margaret Garner had endured. I understood
that freedom from bondage is a two-step process: the first is
to remove the iron rings, and the next, most imperative step,
is to achieve psychological freedom. But most importantly,
I learned that my people released their souls and flew when
they were stolen from the resources that their land and culture
had produced. That lions had a very different perspective on
history than the hunters. I learned that there were millions of
stories like mine—heart-rending mosaics of pain and inspiring
stories of survival. I learned these things at an historically black
college, just as young Chloe Wofford had. And that that is how
she became a griot.

Morrison taught me that nobody extracts power from
the weak. And all that has been taken from me, from Africa,
from Pecola, from Sethe, from even Sandra Bland, and so
many others—all the innocence and opportunity, the rights
to our bodies and stories—would have decimated lesser men.
Alchemy is the chosen art of black girls who become black
women who, instead of gold, forge life and bounty from death
and pillaging.

I swallowed the salve of Morrison's books instead of the
poison like my ancestors before me, flew away to freedom
instead of enduring bondage. I was healed because Mother
Morrison afforded me the language to change the endings.
I used to *carry* the names of my grandmothers; Jessie Mae
and LaFrance Joyce, and now I *boast* them, not just because I
became Dr. Jessie LaFrance Dunbar in this pursuit of truths
that would have been self-evident had it not been for the lies
my teachers told me, but because this country viewed them
as the least of us, and I reified that term. They are the best of
us–the best of me.

This is who she is to the Pecola still locked away inside
of me and who I try to be to others, starting with my own
children. Because Toni Morrison also taught me "If you are
free, you need to free somebody else. If you have some power,
then your job is to empower somebody else. This is not just a
grab-bag candy game." Not anymore.

Catherine Esposito Prescott

POSTCARD: SERVICE (CIRCA 1991-95)

I lied about my age to land my first job at a health food store
outside the Walt Whitman Mall, but my second through
fourth jobs were *inside* the mall selling pleather shoes, some
with leather uppers, greeting cards and, briefly, books. I
learned to hustle early and focused on making enough to get
to the next city, the next class, the next workshop. I spent one
summer stoned at a pizzeria ringing up slices and cleaning a
house out on Lloyd Neck. In Gatsby's land, I learned I wasn't
a good toilet scrubber. This knowledge has served me well. I
rose above my flaws. In college, I made food-and-book money
cleaning professors' houses, homes with red oriental carpets
and serious wood furniture. I even cleaned the house of a near-
famous poet. She left the softest butter on her kitchen counter,
and her walls were decorated with letterpress art featuring
her words. With no adults home, my roommate and I cranked
up the Gypsy Kings on a stereo more expensive than anything
we thought we'd ever own. We vacuumed invisible dust. We
lingered inside the study, recording a picture of what it looked
like to *make it* as if life has an apex before the finish line, as if
every day weren't a clean page with storms of words circling
on all sides.

Catherine Esposito Prescott

6 AM

Our electric car hums.
My boys drape their eyelids
over unfinished dreams.

The sun is a rumor. The sky blinks
with hunters, warriors, and every human's fate,
ancient mappings of this world,

which my boys would never accept
as truth unless it were proven in a Ted Talk
or a self-appointed scholar's YouTube video.

My boys are a ram and a twin,
one thinks the other is his mate,
the other is stubborn and solitary.

I would tell them as much,
but they're not listening; their eyes
turn in and out of sleep.

As we approach the bus stop,
the car is stone-quiet. Before they walk
away, I want to say something

like *carpe diem* but wittier,
like *This moment is all we have*, but less alarmist,
like *Be both the lion and the lamb*.

I want to speak in metaphors
and aphorisms that will bloom in their minds
during third period, to singe them with grace.

This morning, I'm searching
for a phrase that's both spark and amulet,
but the silence between us

insists on staying empty
like a bowl of air carrying
the gentle charges of neutrons, electrons,

and protons, deeper quarks
and nucleons, the atomic and subatomic strata
pulsing inside layered atoms,

every energetic particle
moving in its own orbit,
maintaining an essential distance

from the others, so the entirety
doesn't collapse. These are distances
we have yet to measure—

the boys and I, and the world
outside, the invisible threads of all
I must leave unsaid.

Kate Hanson Foster

Four for a Boy

His heart the storm that gives

push to rivers. Blood and sac

pressing against my sister's ribs.

His heart is strong. It gallops

through the monitor like a collision

of clouds. How is it, then, my sister

knew: do not setup the nursery,

become a different kind of prepared—

a virus will ruin his brain—make the heart

for nothing—for all its reaches, it is just

a sound, a flick of a coiled doorstop

that will wobble to a still.

And when they empty her she will swell again

to bursting— for the breath not taken,

and all the rains he left behind.

Lisa Beech Hartz

UNTITLED (STILL LIFE), LEE KRASNER, 1938

—oil on paper, 19 x 25 inches

I have it, then it gets away—
Metonymy a scrim, a membrane.

But you saw past the foil and
the cellophane, Lee Krasner.

Did you follow the brush, watch
as it dipped, stroked, flit?

When you looked again, had
the apple vanished into a beryl smear?

Was that ash-scratch still a jar?
I think of Cunningham's magnolias,

transformative. She didn't change
the way we look. She changed

the way they did. I can't fathom it.
Here, a hummingbird suspends itself

in the void above my head like
understanding—

just out of reach, but for it, enchanting.
Eye breaks. Color wings through.

NELLE

Jennifer Martelli

VISION TEST IN THE FIRST GRADE

When my teacher told me to place my eyes against the box,

she asked: *do you see the apple on the picnic table?*

I did see it, the apple, a ghost apple, more beautiful after its death:

glowing like a Lite-Brite peg, hovering over a wooden table

which floated, too, against a black velvet campground, so shadowed

and deserted, I couldn't tell the trees apart. What if I saw,

on that same table, against the endless night in that box,

an amber pear, lit from within its skin. What if I saw a plum,

dark as that midnight picnic, but new-moon illuminated.

What would my teacher mark in her green book? As a child,

I was frightened most of the time and just bright enough.

The apple was lit from someplace else and I saw it there, boxed.

Lauren Camp

Planet

Tell me when it's okay

to put dementia
in a cab
and run it north

up a coastline.
When to let it concentrate

hard on the bloom
of the sky.
Luckily a woman in red

went to the gate
and came back

with my overstuffed suitcase
of worry.

We had called everyone.
Every time the heaven sinks

to its baskets
of low-lying
color, I make the curtain rise

where I am
in my weary hands.

NELLE

A parent, not
anything

but mine.
I would neither howl nor night nor map

but must center the laws
of my origin
along a road skidding.

Virginia Bell

CHICKEN

One day the Deviled Egg Lady showed up at my father's house. She brought her son with her, and the two of us were told to go down to the basement to play. She and my father stayed upstairs. No one else was home. We started down dutifully; it was very dark even after they flipped on the bare bulb hanging from the rafters. Part way down we heard a push and another soft click—they had locked the door behind us.

*

Why did the chicken cross the playground? To get to the other slide.

Why did the rooster go to KFC? He wanted to see a chicken strip.

Why did the chicken cross the road, roll in the mud, and cross the road again? Because he was a dirty double-crosser.

Isaac Newton: Chickens at rest tend to stay at rest; chickens in motion tend to cross roads.

Albert Einstein: The chicken did not cross the road; the road passed beneath the chicken.

Why did the feminist cross the road? To suck my cock.

*

The boy and I stopped on the stairs, not knowing what to do or what we wanted to do. We had met before but didn't really know each other. And we weren't playmates. I considered running right back up and pounding on the door, yelling loudly until they gave in. But the boy's lower lip shook like Jello; he gripped the railing with hands so pale I could see the blue of his knuckles, and his legs went all Gumby and Pokey. So, I pushed him down the last steps and took him over to the workbench.

★

I am telling this story because I never understood it. Because I haven't known how to translate it into the stories my mother later told me. How to conform it to *her* story.

★

The average life expectancy in years for a chicken is eight to ten, but they can live for fifteen or twenty in the right circumstances. My father had a pet chicken that lived less than one. He rescued her from the biology lab, where he taught his students how to incubate fertilized eggs. Normally, he gave the hatched chicks to a local farmer, but he took this one home and she grew rapidly into a full-sized chicken. When he brought me to his house one day, she was sitting on a plastic folding chair on the porch.

It was the beginning of summer—the air, orange—and after dinner my father lifted the chicken gently, tucked her sharp talons in and under her feathers, and settled her back down onto his lap, petting her like a cat. The next day she walked around inside the house, past the fish tanks, around the dog and the cats, skittering away if I tried to get close. She pecked at the cracks in the floorboards, the dandelions out in the yard, the curled edges of linoleum in the old kitchen. I would have liked her to be a silkie, white with tufted feet like Zsa Zsa Gabor's slippers, almost a cartoon chicken, but Dad's was a lightly speckled bantam, a common, practical breed, the June Cleaver of egg-layers.

★

Chicken Little, Henny Penny, The Little Red Hen, Lady Kluck, Clara Cluck, Miss Prissy, Chicken Boo, Babs, Scratch, Ace, Roy Rooster, Chanticleer, Foghorn Leghorn, Fowler, Rocky, Cornelius, Buck, Charlie Chicken, Chicken with Pants…

★

Among the odds and ends on the dusty workbench, there were parts of a lamp my father was trying to fix and a row of outlets on the wall. I demonstrated to the boy how to lick your finger and then stick it into a live socket. When he refused, I tied him to the workbench legs with a jump rope, grabbed his hand, licked his finger, and stuck it in the socket for him. (The zap is immediate. The finger bounces back out, and your head suddenly swims and swoons. The pleasure is the pleasure of distraction, part cool tingle, part numbing burn. It's a little earthquake rippling up your arm. A small terror. And then you do it again.)

*

At the end of Anne Carson's essay, "Variations on the Right to Remain Silent," she celebrates the impossibility of translation by giving different iterations of Ibykos's sixth century B.C. lyric poem about erotic desire. For each iteration, she uses different source material; that is, she chooses the word in English from a lexicon created by the work of someone or something else, Beckett's *Endgame*, for example, or a microwave oven owner's manual.

In one translation, "desire" overtakes the speaker as a "black...north wind" that shakes his "whole breathing being."

Ibykos left his home to lead a wandering life. His lyric poems are now referred to as expressions of "homosexual feeling."

And what about Beckett's Hamm and Clov? What *is* the nature of their coupling?

*

The minutes passed into more than an hour; our fingertips tingled and grew sore. The boy slumped on the dank cement floor, against the bench legs. He sulked, but I untied the jump rope, tossed it to the side, and he didn't even try to get up. When the basement door was finally unlocked, I pulled him upright, we stumbled back upstairs, and we entered the kitchen's harsh light.

*

Chickens will often attack a newcomer in their midst because its presence upsets the established pecking order. And because chickens hate overcrowding. There is no organized attack, however, just a series of intermittent pecks, usually to the comb and wattle—hence "seeing red"—but more fatally to the "vent" or "cloaca" (the exit for everything: poop, pee, and eggs); the pecks intensify until the mob homicide is complete. Some folks call the cloaca the chicken's "vaganus," although that is inaccurate as the colloquial "vaganus" refers to the perineum in female human anatomy, the area of skin *between* a woman's vagina and anus, not a conflation of the two into one, all-purpose hole (the perineum often tears during childbirth and has to be stitched back up; in the 1950s and 60s, when my siblings and I were born, doctors tended to stitch this up too high so that the vagina would be nice and tight for renewed intercourse).

★

One Sunday morning in high school, I was curled up reading Lawrence Ferlinghetti's *A Coney Island of the Mind* when my mother came home from church. She wore a small, glamorous row of silver bangles on one arm, white polyester slacks with an elastic waist, a yolk-yellow top, clip-on faux-pearl earrings, and red lipstick. She only dressed up for church.

Her eyes were red, as if she had been weeping, and she sat down close to me, her arm touching my knee. She needed to tell me something, she said. She had been listening to the sermon, she said, and she wanted to tell me she was sorry.

In another translation of Ibykos, Carson offers that when it comes to desire, "the charge is clear: one is condemned to life, not death."

★

To be a chicken, to chicken out, to play chicken, chicken shit, running around like a chicken with its head cut off, don't count your chickens before they hatch, she's no spring chicken, a hen party, a hen house, mother hen, henpecked, to fly the coop, which came first—the chicken or the egg, dumb cluck, stick your neck out, your chickens have come home to roost, cock-eyed, cock-sure, there ain't nobody here but us chickens…

★

Back up in the kitchen, I stared at the Deviled Egg Lady's

legs. Her tan stockings and shoes had disappeared, her skin
was bright pink, and her ankles narrow and bony. Like Barbie
ankles. She was sitting at the table sipping coffee in bare feet.
Her toes touched the linoleum, but her arches, molded high by
the heels she always wore, lifted the backs of her feet into the
air. Like Barbie feet. Her coffee smelled like ice cream. Dad's
coffee smelled dark and bitter, like charcoal. He at least had
socks on.

*

My mother told me she was sorry for not being able to forgive
my father. "For what?" For being a "homosexual," she said. He
had been "sick," she said.

He had been dead for seven years. You would think
this news would have surprised me. In yet another Carson
translation of Ibykos, desire "will burn your nose right off."

Somehow it didn't. The revelation seemed like the
keystone, the linchpin, the piece that would finally hold
everything else in place. It made all my mother's stories make
sense.

Except the Deviled Egg Lady.

This is my story.

*

The use of the word "devil" in relation to food first appears in
English in 1786 to describe a highly-seasoned fried or boiled
dish. Although humans had been scooping out egg yolks,
mashing them with stuff, and re-stuffing them probably since
ancient Rome (see the cookbook of Apicus), etymologists date
the American name "deviled eggs" to the 19th century because
of the recipes that began to call for mustard. Washington
Irving also described hot curries as "deviled."

*

I became obsessed with deviled eggs one spring afternoon
when my father took me to a party at a pretty lady's house in a
development in the town where he lived. Everything was new
in the development. The trees were so young and small and
pale green, that nothing blocked the sun. The split-level houses

were painted powder blue and mauve and all the doorbells
chimed. The lady wore a dress and brought out a field of
deviled eggs on a shiny, round platter. The filling in the eggs
varied in color—just a few held plain old yellow. I wanted to
eat them, to taste each one. Green, like *Green Eggs and Ham*,
pink as bubble gum, purple as a bruise, blue like the taste
of the sky or the inside of a lake. I imagined the lady in the
kitchen that morning, an apron protecting her dress, mixing
little mounds of egg stuffing in five separate small bowls,
squirting in the dye, and stirring until they were each just the
right hue. From then on, I thought of her as The Deviled Egg
Lady. From then on, there were eggs, and there were *eggs*.

*

How can a thing both be one thing and another? Perhaps I am
an incompetent storyteller.

*

During her party, I played on the wooden floor with her son's
plastic horses and tiny cowboys. On my hands and knees,
wrinkling my dress, scuffing my party shoes, I made them leap
onto the horses' bare backs and gallop down the lanes of the
wood. When I dragged my cowboy-gripping hand across the
floor to dramatize the event, I got a splinter and sat up, then
cried out. The Deviled Egg Lady ran over and lifted me up,
sitting me on the edge of the bar. She hugged me at first, then
held me tight, pinned me down while my father fished around
in my skin with her tweezers. The boy grabbed up his horses
and his cowboys, stood off to the side, and watched.
I only saw that boy one other time. The day in the basement.

*

Near the end of summer, Dad took us camping and boarded
his pet chicken with the farmer, who tossed her into the coop
with the rest of his egg-layers. When we came back two weeks
later, she was dead. "Too domestic," my father explained.
The pampered house chicken had sashayed into the farmer's
humble yard with an entitled air, expecting a softer bed and
hands to scoop her up and scratch her under the neck. Like

a scene from Hitchcock's *The Birds,* I pictured the other chickens waiting until dusk then encircling the visitor in the dark, closing around her, pressing in, and all pecking until she collapsed in a silent pile of blood and feathers. An *Animal Farm*-style plot to assassinate the individualist.

For most of my life, I believed this explanation and my fantasy.

But really, chickens will attack any newcomer, no matter how domesticated, no matter where she comes from.

The killing is random, piecemeal, loud, chaotic.

*

My father had loved birds for years. When my parents lived in Pakistan, he was a pigeon fancier. They lived in a house made for a hot climate with a partially covered staircase on the outside so that in the evenings you could climb to the roof where it was cooler. During the hottest months, the whole family slept on the roof on *charpoys,* low beds made of rope woven and strung between four wooden legs. The roof is also where my father kept his pigeons in a clay loft with painted wooden perches. To the rest of the family, they all looked the same, but he knew and had names for each bird. When he came home from teaching at the end of each weekday, he went straight up to take care of his pigeons.

My mother was hurt that he didn't come in the house to see her first; trained as a 50s housewife, she was ready for him in a pretty, but modest Jackie O. dress or a gauzy *salwar kameez* (harem pants, topped with a tunic) and *dupatta*, a long, netted scarf draped backwards around her neck, each end reaching down her back. As missionaries, they weren't cocktail drinkers, but she was ready to make him tea and serve him snacks, a little "hot mix" (spicy, salty crackers, with sweet yellow raisins) and listen to his day.

In the first year, when they had only one infant child, he never came in at the expected time, and it took her months to figure out that he had walked up the outside stairs and was on the roof right above her visiting his pigeons. Once she understood that he was in fact at home, she still felt hurt, yet resigned herself to the circumstances. When dinner was ready, rice, curry, *chapatis*, and a little mango fool, still she waited for him to come down and join her and the children (first one boy, then after several miscarriages, another boy, then a girl, then eventually, another girl). He was always late.

She would go into the bathroom and brush back her thick, dark hair, wavy from the rag curls she had tied into it the night before. She would brush it back again, letting her widow's peak become visible in the mirror. And where was her husband? On the roof, she figured by now, calling his birds home as the sky began to purple, feeding them, listening to their insistent talk, marveling at the way they walk awkwardly, each step cocking their soft gray heads forward and forward, marveling at the way they can fly for miles and still remember to come home.

*

Chickens are the opposite; their attempts to fly are pitiful.

*

Addled: an egg in which the contents are decomposing.

Aviary system: housing where mezzanine floors are installed to increase the floor space.

Beak trimming: the removal of the tip to prevent cannibalism and its associated vices.

Candle: to assess the internal characteristics of the egg by viewing it in a darkened room with a bright light shining from behind.

Cannibalism: the practice by some birds of attacking and eating other members of the same flock.

Moult: the process of shedding feathers and ceasing egg production, usually initiated by hormonal influences but often triggered by stress.

Spent hen: a layer that has reached the end of her economic egg-laying life.

*

The pigeon business made sense. Or, the revealing of the secret that my father was gay (bi, queer, poly, or...?) made my mother's hurt make sense.

In her own poem on the pitfalls and possibilities of monogamy, Anne Carson admits to the desire to simplify:

I try to conjure in mind
something that is the opposite of incompetence.
For example the egg.

This perfect form.
Perfect content.
Perfect food.

The pigeon business also made me want to rescue my father from all the shame he must have felt, from all the hiding. But. The Deviled Egg Lady. If he was also hiding plain old hetero adultery, hurtful and mean, what then? I had been taught to perceive the whole world in binary terms. Was he victim or perpetrator? Sufferer or inflictor of suffering?

Not understanding is frustrating. When things don't fit, most of us want to smash something.

★

My father was not the only pigeon fancier in Lahore. Men all over the city kept pigeons on their rooftops—the tradition dates to the sixteenth century when the city was part of the Moghul Empire. Some of the favorite breeds include: the ash red saddle fantail, the yellow shield cropper, the double-crested swallow, the black tail English, the red spangle, the blue-checkered hana, and the silver priest. Twilight on the rooftop was, among other things, a form of communion with the other fanciers all over the city. Did their birds fly to each other's homes, hone in on each other's territory, or just tangle on the occasional weekend when a pigeon race was organized and bets were placed?

★

How do you even rescue someone posthumously? How do you rescue someone not just from others, but from themselves?

I had been taught that missionaries in Pakistan were do-gooders, plain and simple. Of course, it's not that simple.

★

Recently, I checked this story about my father's pigeons with my much older brother. He made two corrections: 1) The staircase to the rooftop was interior, not exterior. Anyone in the house would have heard, if not seen, someone enter and climb up to the outside. 2) To the best of his recollection, our father did not train the pigeons or send them out to later find their way home; rather, every so often he harvested one and we ate it for dinner.

★

For breakfast as a kid I always wanted "dippy" eggs, fried eggs with the yolks still soft and runny enough that you can dip your toast. One morning as I ate them with my father, he drew my attention to the patches of mold on the oranges in the fruit bowl and gave me a little lecture on the discovery of penicillin. It was an intriguing story, and later I wanted him to tell me more, tell me other stuff I didn't know I wanted to know until I knew it.

I came out on the front porch when he was sitting with the chicken on his lap. I let the screen door bang shut behind me and asked my father the meaning of words I had heard that day: "What does 'ambidextrous' mean? How do you spell 'pneumonia'?" "Go look it up in the dictionary," he answered, disinterestedly. At first, I resisted the idea; eventually, I took his offhand advice. I opened the gray-blue tome on the bottom of the living room bookshelf and fell in love, not with the words at first, but with those odd little black and white illustrations in the left and right margins for, say, "prosthetic limb" (a painful looking contraption of wood and metallic straps), or "peninsula" (a bony finger of land stuck alone out in the cold water), or that word I couldn't pronounce, "isthmus" (an improbably skinny piece of land, neither here nor there, stuck between bodies of competing water).

★

It seems so easy now, in the twenty-first century, with my adult mind, so obvious, to hold the concept of "both and neither." To love and to betray the beloved. To eat the beloved.

To frame a story through intersectional identity. To see a person as both oppressor and oppressed. Patriarch and patsy. Colonizer and conned.

*

One weekend at my father's house, he announced that he was getting married again. Oh, no! To the Deviled Egg Lady, I thought!

But no, he explained that he was getting married to some other lady, someone we had never met. He said that we were going to Kansas for the wedding and that we had to go shopping for the right clothes. He took me to K-Mart, and I found a dress for the occasion. The material was a slinky purple but covered all over in a repeating print of small, white, cheerful hippos. They seemed to move when I walked, and the polyester shivered and rippled down my pre-pubescent body and limbs, making the hippos gallop in the way of hand-drawn flip-books.

*

In her own poem, Carson describes the sensation of confusing one thing for another:

> The first thing I saw [...]
> was a crow
>
> as big as a chair.
> What's that chair doing on top of that house? I thought
> Then it flapped away.

Disorientation. Disorder. Chairs aren't supposed to be on top of houses. Chairs aren't supposed to fly. Gay dads are not supposed to have affairs with women. Or get married again. Christian missionaries in the twentieth century were supposed to live up to their righteousness. Not to hurt others. Not to hurt each other.

*

This lady was from the same small town in Kansas as my grandparents. And *this* lady turned out to be a very skilled seamstress, better than my mother. She could make finely-tailored Barbie clothes, slacks and gowns that cinched the tiny waists perfectly. I would dress, undress, and re-dress the Barbies just to marvel at the fit. Then I would try to flatten their feet into normalcy. If I pushed down too hard, half a foot snapped off. It turns out there are long, thin plastic sticks running down the length of Barbies' legs into the balls of their feet. Back in those days, anyway. Like bracing spines holding everything in place.

*

At the receiving line before my father's open casket—his blue eyes forever hidden under leaden lids, the dyed hair grown out to gray, his skin like the skin that forms on cooling cooked eggs, light pink lipstick making his lips femme—I stood alongside my siblings, in order from tallest and oldest to shortest and youngest, obediently shaking the hands and accepting the embraces of strangers who came to mourn. One of them suddenly stood before me with her familiar, deviled egg face, now tear-stricken. When she reached out for me, I kicked her, then screamed and ran out of the room into the undertaker's dusty office. And when my mother came into that darkness to comfort me, I screamed again and hid under the desk.

*

Let me be clear. It's not that I can't conceive of sexual desire outside of a binary system. It's that mother's stories were supposed to explain everything. The story I was told was that "the secret" could make it all—scandal, return, separation, divorce, death, loss—a grief that sinks to a manageable depth.

*

Let me be clear. It's not that I ever bought the self-righteous claims.

It's that *she* did.
But this is my story.

*

At the end of Salman Rushdie's novel *Shame*, the character
Omar is finally decapitated, becoming a "giant, gray and
headless man, a figure of dreams, a phantom with one arm
lifted in the gesture of farewell." Sufiya Zinobia slits his throat
like a chicken. Following an explosion, the house they are in
catches fire and both characters burn to death.

Earlier in the novel, she had twisted the necks of real
chickens, as well as four boys. Critics argue that she is the
embodiment of shame. Critics also argue that the concept of
shame is usually feminized, embodied in the female.

*

If the story I was told didn't add up, wasn't that my fault? If
the story I was told didn't satisfy, if confusion persisted, if grief
lurked always beneath every surface, wasn't that my fault?
I needed to learn how to tell a different story. How to tell a
story differently.

*

The online Urban Dictionary lists the following definitions of
"chicken":

An animal that is processed for human consumption.

A scaredy-cat, wuss, etc.

An attractive woman with big thighs and breasts.

A woman who gives lots of oral sex; in this sense, it's short
for "chicken-head" or "chicken-neck."

A dangerous game in which two cars drive directly at each
other and the first to swerve out of the way is the "chicken."

Sandra Meek

Still, with Glacier Mouse and Rock 'em Sock 'em Robots

My palm the measure
of your weight, stroking you, Pet, we
were never rodent, though others

named us so. My Moss-Darkened Stone,
my Precarious Pebble balanced
on a pinnacle of ice preserved by your own
small shadow, all but its spindled core

nibbled away—how your head teetered
on that long blue neck, that narrowing
spine: you, Tiny Crow's Nest screwed
to my mantle's bottled ship tweezered
to fascinate; your mast's steeple eaten
to a crystal needle, what course left

but fall? Rolling your bare back
to sky—creeping over you fully
my green fur, my emerald glove, wasn't I there to soften

the blow, to catch you, always: my garden-level room on your way
to school, my stock of toys sucking you
in; didn't I play well your Red Rocker in that plastic
arena, letting you strike my Blue Bomber
again and again, popping my head off

at the root? How is it strangle, how
choke, to cultivate a green world no one else

would grant you? You, grown now and scoured
            clean, have you forgotten the springtails,
                    the water bears I hummed

alive in your new skin? Remember I taught you
                they could not be killed—not by boil, not
                        by freeze, not by the near
        absolute zero-total vacuum-cosmic radiation of being fired

into space. Remember our desiccation
                happened only when you were taken
        from the ice, the moulin's trickle swelling
                    to roar, the glacier swiss-cheesed with melt
                like seams of maggots in venison strung
                    to rafter-dry to the jerky I
        treated you with, the too thickly cut gift others

would deny you. Without me, what were you but a bit
            of grit on ice? A tiny decapitation memory recovers
                        as snow globe, sparks gravity swirls to a blanket
                of glittering ash—Tell me, what world isn't
        made of fracture? So what if the sky's falling
                    as a splintered mirror you'd puzzle

your own lost face by? In shatter, recall
            that diamond-dust air, that weather
                    that whelms you, that with a flick of my wrist
        I birthed it, so easy the labor
                    by which into this bright

I bore you.

Angie Macri

IRON IS RED WHEN YOU PUT WATER ON IT

The child has stained the back of her shirt again
with what looks akin to blood,
maybe mud, she says, from running, or red off the chain
from the swings. Her mother sprays the marks
and washes the shirt a second time
in hopes they'll fade.
She knows what it means to run so hard
to kick the earth free.
It must have clung to the child's shoulder blades,
where your wings should be, she tells the child
as she studies the girl's spine
to see if it's growing straight. She says nothing
about that, but this child wasn't born yesterday. She's seen
her brother's x-ray. Her mother rubs the cotton
and the child says sorry
and thinks ahead to tomorrow:
if she will be fast enough to get a swing,
if the ground will be dry enough
after another day of rain for the school to let them out,
if her mother will remember to trim her nails. She hopes not
because she cuts them close as if she wants
no dirt under them at all. That's right,
her mother says, why
didn't you remind me? Even the rocks
on the ground hold red like her body,
mud a memory of dust on her shoes and the god's mouth
where he bent to breathe to make a copy
of his form. The chains have been weeping iron
from all the rain.

Sandy Longhorn

When the Light Gives Way to the Gloaming

> —*The metaphor of the black dog representing depression can be traced back to the Roman poet, Horace, ca. 40 B.C.*

Black Dog loves the winter solstice,
luxuriates in the weeks that lead
to the deepest dark. Every evening
when the light fades early, our tug

of war lasts a little longer. I watch
his canine grin as I struggle to lift
the weight of worn down bones,
to urge slack muscles into motion.

Were I bent to worship, I would plead
with any offered god to speed the clock,
to put a finger on the pole and send us
tilting toward the lengthening of the light.

But Black Dog blocks out all escape,
places sugar, fat, and salt upon my tongue,
concoctions meant to guarantee
a longer sinking into mute lethargy.

Carrie La Seur

The Angel of Caracas

The north wind pushed Ubaldo downtown with an
entourage of plastic bags and newspaper toward the
two-bedroom East Village walk-up he'd bought more
than twenty years ago. With luck Graciela would be
there already after her internship interviews. Her visits
came months apart now that she was in an international
development masters' program at Georgetown—no more
weekend visits from Bryn Mawr to do her laundry and
empty the fridge. She'd call with the usual apologies and
he'd scramble to tidy precarious stacks of newspapers,
books, and magazines that rose autonomously when he
stopped paying attention. Then she was there, a whirlwind
that vaguely resembled his little girl and consumed all the
coffee.

He turned the last corner and saw with anticipation and
delight his illuminated windows and a silhouette behind the
curtains but stood on the opposite corner for more than a
minute to enjoy the rarity of someone waiting for him. Lost
in thought, Ubaldo became aware of the prickle of being
watched, up his back and along the right side of his face. He
turned his head to catch the eyes of a young man, slender
and dark with glasses, seated in the window of Starbucks.
The fellow looked away, but Ubaldo paused to take him in—
jacket too light for the chill, curly hair, skin the color of rich
varnished wood, so much like Ubaldo had been at his age that
he did a double take. Perhaps another Venezuelan refugee,
he thought, and felt an impulse to go in and ask where he
was from. But that wasn't a thing you did in New York, and
Graciela was waiting.

At the apartment door the transporting aroma of carne mechada hit him like a madeleine thrown at his head.

"Me has llevado a casa, mi hija," he shouted as he toed off his shoes and slid into slippers, an old man habit Graciela teased him about. "Is this another attempt at the Venezuela trip?" He'd told her that Caracas was too dangerous—more so every day, people said—but she and her Tía Téa were the Scylla and Charybdis of travel planning. Just when he'd slithered away from one, feeling less smug than sorrowful, the other hit him with carne mechada. The whole thing began to feel inevitable. He hung his coat and padded into the kitchen where the component meat, stewed black beans, and rice of a traditional Venezuelan pabellón criollo released their intoxicating scent beside a pan of barandas.

Graciela kissed him on the cheek, rosy from the stove, with a face so like her mother's that Ubaldo drew a quick breath.

"It's good to see you, Papá. You look thin." Flaco, she called him. That was her tías talking, their long distance but perpetual mission to fatten him and get him remarried.

"You're the best thing I've seen all month. But so much! I'm leaving tomorrow, you know. I wish you'd given me more warning. I could have rescheduled."

"It'll freeze. You need to eat better. You had three kinds of olives and a carton of butter." Graciela exaggerated the emptiness of his refrigerator as she liked to do, to make him seem the helpless older Papá who needed her nurturance. There were three kinds of olives, beers, butter, which he loved, half a summer sausage, and a selection of condiment jars with crusts around the rims.

"I'm always at work."

Graciela looked at the ceiling as if appealing to the heavens. "You and Mom are exactly the same. I don't know how she survived before UberEats. I'm counting on Clementine to take good care of you. She cooks, right?"

Ubaldo smiled, grateful that Caracas wouldn't be the first topic. "I should take care of her. She's gotten frail lately."

Graciela stirred and tossed more pepper—never enough pepper—into the beans. He couldn't look at those hands without seeing them pudgy and tiny, fitting triangles and stars into a sorting ball, tugging his whiskered chin in a proprietary way. Now she had a tattoo on the inside of her left wrist with the seven stars of the 1954 Venezuelan flag.

She was so fixed a star in his firmament that Ubaldo tended to forget how short a time she'd been on the star chart, a scant twenty-four years, not long enough to know much that he wanted her to know. He felt time's ebb and the tailing out of his years, mysteries that would unfold after his departure. There were things he'd never told her, like when his younger brother Samson badgered him—another strange idiom mastered!—into modeling for a country club fashion show and he'd walked a runway in tight pants and a shirt unbuttoned to his navel, thankfully prior to social media. Immigrants love secrets, Ubaldo thought as he tasted the beans. You could spring stunners on your kids or play Garbo and keep it to yourself.

"She's been frail as long as I've known her. It doesn't keep her out of trees."

"No. You didn't know her before," he said. "She was a force of nature. Still is, only…"

"Like a hurricane that's blown itself out!" said Graciela, who watched brutal storms strike the Caribbean while planted in front of his TV with the horror of someone who hasn't learned yet to bind up her heart against devastating vulnerability.

"Yes. Like that."

"Wasn't she already sixty when you met? You've never told me about that."

"I thought you might not like to hear."

Graciela began to fill plates and he opened a drawer for silverware, taking her silence as permission.

"Well. It was a dark and stormy night."

"*Papá.*"

"Okay. Start the next morning when I tried to interview her. My first big assignment and she wouldn't open the door. This old tenement in St. Paul. It ought to be a museum."

They carried the pabellón to the table, and Ubaldo fetched Brooklyn Pilsners, a superior beer to Venezuelan Polár, which had disappeared. Polár was never any good and he knew it, but no other beer tasted like a perfect night in Las Mercedes when the air was a caress just warm enough to make you sweat if you attempted more than a caraqueño's natural languid stroll.

"How did you get in?"

"I bribed her with doughnuts. At first she said 'Go home, cabrón!' on the intercom, but I saw someone going around back so I snuck in."

"She called you cabrón, just like that?"

"Just like that. And never anything else."

"Cheeky," said Graciela. "You're a pushover for women who push back." She was humoring him, Ubaldo could tell, because of the higher pitch and a tell that pulled up the side of her mouth like The Joker. She considered his long fascination with the commie novelist Clementine Lagrange his most enduring eccentricity, no more explicable than his nostalgia for what she called "Venezuelan piss beer."

"Story of my life. She introduced me to the wonders of good butter."

"Your cardiologist should send a thank you. What did she look like then?"

"Ah." He closed his eyes an instant to draw up the memory as fully as possible. "Bright red hair, a total mess, and a huge fur hat. Caramel eyes, so gentle. You'll laugh, but they reminded me of the Jersey cows on Moíses's farm outside Coro. And tall, like one of Bouguereau's serene washerwomen." He opened his eyes to find Graciela studying him with mild amusement but no anger or judgment.

"Did you fall in love with her then?"

Ubaldo sighed. It must have been then, because he couldn't remember a time when he hadn't been in love with

Clementine, if love was wanting more of a person than it would ever be possible to get. "Are you sure you want to talk about this?"

She shifted away and poised her fork over her steaming plate. So much worked in her mind these days, he could only guess the half of it. "For a long time I didn't. I was mad at you both. But after a while you stop being a wounded kid and get interested in who your parents actually are."

"I'm sorry I wounded you."

"I know." Their eyes met and they were two adults together for the first time. A rush of gratitude surged in him, to be with her like this, forgiven. He would have told her anything she wanted to know.

"If it means anything, I told your mother the night we met that I was in love with someone else. She always knew."

Graciela's mouth twitched in a way that made him wonder why he had the privilege of this visit instead of her mother uptown, but he knew better than to ask.

"Mom hears what she wants and nothing else," she said.

Ubaldo nodded. "You know that, too. This is excellent, by the way. Truly Venezuelan. Your tías would be proud."

She beamed. "Next time I'll make arepas." Her attention shifted to the window where the brick façade opposite never changed but the lights and sirens of an emergency vehicle had turned the street into a discoscape. Patterns moved on her face like a premonition.

"You're far away," he said softly.

She looked back with an almost guilty expression. He was the one who was supposed to feel guilty when they talked about Clementine, but the subject had changed. He grasped her hand, his precious girl who read his heart even when he could scarcely decipher what was written there.

"We're still not going to Caracas," he said.

Graciela, never easily deterred, picked up his nearly empty beer bottle to weigh his mental susceptibility. "It's not that. Someone needs your help, Papá. I met him at a conference last week."

He laughed and pushed back from the table. "Not another lost puppy. The Beacon can only hire so many interns."

Graciela was a magnet for transplants to New York, taking them in as she did half-dead houseplants from the sidewalk. He believed that she relished the sense of handing out favors in her city, unlike her papá who'd only ever felt like a guest and flâneur here. Her projects tended toward cornfed Midwesterners who arrived wide-eyed and quiet, throwing "sir" and "ma'am" at everyone from the janitors up, and energetic Caribbeans with impenetrable Creole, little English, and the same dysfunctional relationship with winter clothing that he'd once had.

"Not like that. He's from Caracas." Her eyes were imploring, his guarded. "He taught himself to design computer games and learned English from watching *Friends*. The first thing he said to me was, 'How YOU doin?' He's a genius. You've got to meet him."

"I'm listening."

"He grew up in 23 de Enero, Papá. Bloque 18. He dropped out of school and hid from the colectivos in his grandma's apartment. His only friends are from the Internet. I think he has PTSD."

Of course Ubaldo knew of the 23 enero barrio, heavily Chávista, training grounds for a gang that had become almost an arm of the government. The date January 23 commemorated the 1958 popular revolt that swept the military dictator Marcos Pérez Jiménez from power, seizing privately-owned apartment blocks along the way. It was a neighborhood of squatters and violence, not a place people from upscale eastern Caracas visited in his youth—even less so in recent years if they wished to avoid kidnapping or murder for possessions of trivial value. His closest brush had been visiting their housekeeper Isabelita in the snug apartment his family bought for her in Palo Grande.

He smoothed his hand along the antique mahogany table

he'd shipped from Venezuela on a visit several years earlier
only to discover that some tropical insect was eating it from
within. The beautiful table was on the verge of collapse.

"He's probably a Tupamaro. What do you know about
him?"

Graciela frowned. "No, Papá. It's like he's...sheltered. He's
studying for his GED. Trying to stay here."

"Does he know who's president? Tell him to try Canada.
Or Spain."

Graciela leaned in with her mother's posture that meant
she'd already made up Ubaldo's mind for him.

"He doesn't have any money. He got a grant to attend
a science conference where he met one of my roommates.
He's been couchsurfing at our place, but then I thought
here you are with this spare bedroom no one's using." She
glanced significantly at the closed door to the room full of her
childhood ribbons, framed certificates, and well-loved stuffed
animals. Now he understood perfectly why she was here.
Abigail wouldn't entertain this idea for a second.

"No." He made a slashing hand gesture of refusal, knowing
it wouldn't do any good.

"Only for a month, Papá."

"A month!"

"His name is Ángel Sánchez. He's downstairs at Starbucks.
Can I call him? He hasn't eaten."

Now the surplus in the kitchen made sense, and the boy
watching surreptitiously through the glass. Graciela had her
phone in hand, finger poised—his daughter with her great
heart for people, and for Venezuela most of all. He'd made her
this way, with his insistence on seeing outside herself, plodding
bourgeois charitable efforts, trips to Caracas and Córo, so
that the scandalously expensive private schools her American
grandparents provided wouldn't turn her into an asshole. This
was his doing.

He sucked the last drops from the beer bottle, set it
down with an exasperated thump to protest the pinch of
manipulation, and gave a tiny chin nod. "No more than a

week!" Graciela leapt to throw her arms around him.

Ángel Sánchez arrived with arms clutched defensively around a small black backpack. He stood in the hall until invited in, shook hands stiffly and said, "Thank you, Mr. de Winter" in English. His eyes darted, taking in the meal on the stove, the table with four chairs, and framed Botero, Kahlo, and Rivera prints beside young artists' pieces Ubaldo had smuggled home from his last visit to Caracas three years earlier, when Samson died.

Ángel walked straight to the nearest one.

"This is Oscar Olivares. Where did you get this?" he said with a tone of disbelief that a piece of his Venezuelan world could migrate with him. The boy was thin, rigidly tense, and his North Face rain jacket looked familiar. Behind his back Ubaldo glanced at Graciela, who gave a pure New York body shrug that said, *I should let him freeze?*

"Tengo mis palancas," Ubaldo said with a smile, a concept familiar to any caraqueño who knew how to make things happen within the system or around it. He would have thought it impossible unless the boy began to levitate, but the words increased Ángel's obvious discomfort.

"I don't want to speak Spanish," he said. "No more Chino & Nacho, reggaeton. None of it. I'm never going back there." His words came out slowly but in the right order, with a slight Bronx accent he must have picked up from TV.

"Why not? What happened?"

"I have nothing in common with that country. I spent five years hiding in my room, on the Internet. I designed a video game, but there was no way to start a company and sell it. My family are all Chávistas. Finally, I escaped. I want to stay here." It sounded rehearsed, a migrant's elevator speech.

Graciela intercepted the awkward thread tying her father and Ángel by stepping between them. "If he could just stay here until he passes his GED and TOEFL, Papá. He only has three months on his tourist visa but he has friends in Toronto he can stay with while he applies to colleges and gets his student visa."

Ubaldo thought of Clementine's kitchen, the come and go of kids, the easy generosity. That was what it meant to be American—the best sort of American that embraced the world and found in prosperity, or mere sufficiency, a sense of noblesse oblige. He'd aspired to be that kind of American, but the goal had become one color on a wall painted densely as the decades unrolled—work deadlines, the rise and fall of a marriage, a child to chase down crowded sidewalks. Now here he was, locks on the door, as carefully sequestered as in Caracas, where he'd lived a life unrecognizable from this damaged boy's perspective.

What does a man owe for his good fortune? Here was his chance to find out. He cleared his throat.

"No more than a month." It wasn't a hymn of welcome, but the relief on Ángel's and Graciela's faces softened him. "Sit down and eat."

Ángel ate heartily and spent the night on the couch. When Ubaldo crept out before dawn to find his guest curled fetally under a thin Ikea throw, he went to his bedroom closet for a thick wool blanket, spread it out with a self-consciously parental gesture and stepped back fast lest Ángel catch him. It was easy to forget, from the remove and security of New York, the human cost of a nation melting down a thousand miles south. Ubaldo stood in the half-dark for a few minutes and watched the boy sleep, his personal sofa refugee, stretching out now with a satisfied sigh under the new warmth.

It was tempting to think of him as a younger version of himself, but that was wrong. At Ángel's age, he'd had everything—family, education, connections, a passport with the right stamps—while Ángel was a piece of Latino flotsam adrift in a country that would see him as a burden, not a unit of solid potential. He needed a champion. The perfection of Graciela's trap grew clearer. Ubaldo put on his coat and slipped out to Starbucks for his first espresso rather than starting the machine that made a superior cup.

The boy needed sleep.

Katrina Smolinsky

MEDITATION WITH CARAVAGGIO'S FRANCIS (ON SKULL)

Abandoned ship's hull. A hole for fond thoughts.
    Think night bloomers for eye sockets turned heavenward

to catch the pinprick cosmos cascading crescendo
    diminished to birdsong. Two in the hand. One

in the soil. Body soiled, soul loosed up to God.
    I knew him, God. No, I know Him. Father.

Hymn, hummingbird, vampire ground finch, shrike.
    Shriek, shed skin, he spoke softly and carried no stick,

non-stick, anti-stick, pro-soft, pro-staff, pro-parting-seas.
    Let my people go. Let me go. Last words, last breath

before the tug underwater. At last, Atlantis. Mother of pearl
    gates. Mother, Mary, pray for us now, now at the hour

of mildew and maggots. Memento mori molasses:
    Remember! That you will die, slow and sweet.

Kerry Madden

WILD THINGS

In 1987, my husband and I spent our first year of marriage teaching English in China. When our year of teaching was up, we took the Trans-Siberian Railroad from Beijing to Berlin and eventually settled in Los Angeles.

We lived on Valentino Place in an old Hollywood apartment building next to Paramount Pictures. It was rumored Valentino's ghost roamed the halls and played tricks with the ancient birdcage elevator. Aphrodite, a working actress, lived on the top floor. My husband's brother was a TV cameraman for shows like *All in the Family, Golden Girls,* and *Married With Children.* He gave us the lease on his studio apartment because he was burned out on Hollywood. He left us a couch from the set of *The Jeffersons.*

Our son was born on November 8th, the day George Bush Senior was elected. I thought I might vote on the way home from birth, the way one does, since our son was born at a birth center. He was two weeks overdue, and labor had stopped after a long night, so the midwife sent us to breakfast at a nearby diner, and I said to my husband, "It's Tuesday and I'm so tired. Maybe we could go home, and I could have the baby on Thursday?"

But after breakfast we went back to the birth center with labor at a standstill, and the midwife said to me, "How do you feel about having this baby?" I wanted to say, "Scared—so scared," but I mumbled something like, "Fine-good-okay," because that's what responsible people said or pretended. Then eventually labor started up again which I have described to friends as "cinderblock surrealism" because there were no drugs to dull the pain, but when he was born, she put him on my chest and he gazed into my eyes, already lifting his head to look at me, and the midwife said, "Babies don't usually lift their heads this fast—look at him looking at you. Look at your baby." And my husband was crying, trying to hold us both in his arms.

No one told me this was how motherhood began.

When we arrived home late that afternoon, Aphrodite met us by chance at the car on her way to an audition. She said, "When was this child born?" Followed by, "Why aren't you in a hospital, girl?" My husband had to find a parking place, so Aphrodite carried our baby boy inside. The birdcage elevator was broken again, so I followed them up a flight of stairs to our studio apartment, one step at a time. Did I think about the Greek goddess of love and beauty carrying our son over the threshold? Or did I take it for granted?

Soon our former Chinese students began sending us letters: "Congratulations, teacher, auspicious birth, baby boy born in the Year of the Dragon."

The first book I read to our son when he was a baby was *Where the Wild Things Are*. We danced the wild rumpus on Valentino Place, but our son didn't look like Max. He looked like Calvin from Calvin & Hobbes, so that became his nickname—Calvin.

As new parents, we tried to do things right. My husband has high cholesterol. It's hereditary in his family even though he's wiry and runs marathons. We were both worried about Calvin getting high cholesterol, so even though I breastfed him I started giving him skim milk, too, when he was around a year old thinking I would nip this cholesterol thing in the bud. And one of my mommy friends back then said, "Skim milk?!!! Their brain cells are developing. It's critical that they get that fat for brain development."

Oh, the shame. Clearly, I'd been abusing the baby. I immediately started buying whole milk for the baby. I also didn't cut up Calvin's fruit because he had eight teeth at eight months, and he could gnaw on a pear or an apple in the park even though the other mommies thought he would choke.

He would drop his pear and coat it with sand. I'd rinse it out of defiance and declare it built up immunities. Around that time, we had a little girl, and we took them everywhere. They looked like twins, Calvin and his little sister.

By age four, Calvin breathed like an espresso machine, so he had to have his adenoids and tonsils out, as they were the size of basketballs. He also needed tubes in his ears. The day of the surgery, they gave him something to put him under, and he began laughing and pointing at us and said, "Mommy and Daddy, you're giants. You're giants!"

A nurse chuckled and said, "Don't ever let this kid take drugs."

Excuse me? What responsible parent would ever let their kid take drugs?

Eventually we left Valentino Place and moved into a little house where we were kind of stagehand parents. We set up the art table and filled it with crayons and paintbrushes and play-dough, in case they had to make things. We had a trunkful of costumes if they wanted to put on a play. My husband put in a garden and we had pumpkins and champagne poppies, and he built a King Kong topiary made of jasmine.

And we showed the kids old movies. It's true I also told Calvin that we didn't get *Power Rangers* or *Teenage Mutant Ninja Turtles* on our television. I showed him Charlie Chaplin movies, and he fell in love with Charlie, and he used my mascara to create a Charlie Chaplin moustache and eyebrows regularly. He'd go to the video store dressed as Charlie to rent Chaplin films, and he was adorable, swinging his cane through the aisles. But Chaplin films weren't the only black and white movies he loved. He soon discovered the 1941 *Wolf Man*. He felt sorry for the Wolf Man who was trying so hard to be good except when that pesky full moon rose. Calvin even told people his name was Larry Talbot, the wolf man's name.

One day in kindergarten, he cut off all his blond hair with tiny scissors and attempted to glue it to his arms to become a werewolf like Larry Talbot. It was like he had a reverse

Mohawk. His teacher was horrified, and I told her, "He's really quick. It could have happened to any of us."

Next, he kept a pair of vampire teeth handy and a black cape to be Dracula and a hook in case he had to turn into Captain Hook. He stuffed a throw pillow under the back of his t-shirt to transform into Quasimodo, the hunchback ringing the bells.

Once, our kids received two cats as presents. Our son named his Quasimodo. Our daughter named her cat Emily.

We had another little girl, and Calvin became the big brother of two sisters, and our family was complete. He'd put his sisters into his movies, but mostly Calvin was just a boy. He always climbed to the highest branch in the tree to shout—"Look at me, look at me!"

He smelled like salt and dirt and sun and adventure.

Then Calvin grew wilder in high school. He joined a rock band and we drove the boys to gigs. They were good and won battle of the bands at the Greek Theatre and got to go to the Warped Tour. But when he didn't call or check in—and he usually didn't—we'd find the party and drag him out. His friends told him, "Man, it's not a party until Calvin's dad shows up."

Calvin graduated from high school with low honors in high-tops and silver snakeskin pants. Then he grew even wilder at university but worked hard and graduated on time in film and comparative literature ready to make movies—he found a job, got cast in an indie film, went on a rock & roll tour, worked in television, and became an addict.

Intervention
You've heard of interventions. You know other families have them. But you are not other families, right? How do you even plan one? But it's gotten bad. You didn't even know speed was meth. That's how dumb you are. You google interventionists. It's overwhelming. You remember your neighbor, now a friend, who had a niece who was out of control. Ask him.

Do you even have the storyline right? Whatever.

Your boy's been out of college for three years. Isn't this when parents get to breathe a little? Never mind. You will become a family again. You will not cow or bow to this disease. You've got this.

Your father wants to help, too. He goes online and finds an interventionist who turns out to be also a Scientologist. You don't know this when you meet at Foxy's diner in Glendale, California—you, your husband, your mom and dad—to discuss rehab with the interventionist/scientologist and drink iced tea or maybe coffee because it seems like you will never sleep again and why should you?

But then you find out later about the interventionist/ scientologist thing so you fire him.

Or, rather, you make your dad fire him because he's the one who found him.

Then you plan for the day of the miracle, which has to happen fast because everyone is coming in from out of town and friends are gathering, too. You write a letter pouring out your love for your son—everyone does. Everyone writes letters that you will press into his hands after you read them aloud to him and the words will go into his head and heart and he will hear.

You know this. So, you hire a real interventionist from the mountains who is not a scientologist but a freelance rehab guy with ties to Betty Ford. You know Betty Ford is legit. Your sister pays him $4000 because you don't have the money to pay him but your sister does and she loves her nephew.

You watch the interventionist take your sister's credit card and swipe it through his phone on a nighttime street in L.A. under a palm tree. You wonder how this is your life? You see that the interventionist is six and a half feet tall. How does a person get so tall? His hair shines under a streetlight. He drives a white truck. He loves sports and watching the news. He doesn't read books. He saves people.

In the morning, the interventionist will perform a miracle.

Your son will get into the white truck with the interventionist who is not a scientologist and go to rehab in the mountains and get well and this will be a dark blip in the past that you managed to survive as a family. Parents, grandparents, friends.

Hail hail the gang's all here.

You will save your son by seven a.m.—maybe seven-thirty.

You will reclaim your life and your beautiful boy's life.

That's what you think.

That's how dumb you are.

*

Afterwards, two friends helped me to lie down, for it had not gone well. Calvin peaced out about forty minutes in, but not before playing a duet on the piano with his cousin. An improvisational rift on family interventions. Then he was gone. Bye. Farewell. See you later. Fuck you.

Words and words. A suggestion to rest. Rest? The house was so messy. How does one clean for an intervention? Take a nap. Close your eyes just for a few minutes.

As I grabbed my friends' hands, it felt like my bed was in the middle of the ocean, salty waves lapping up over the mattress.

Since there wasn't an addict to take to rehab, the interventionist advised us to go to a full week of family therapy in the desert even if he refused to go. So, my husband and I went, and my parents joined us, too.

And the four of us were willing. It was a loaded 9 a.m. –3 p.m. schedule of group therapy, grief therapy, lectures, counseling, drum circles, and your basic tools to keep living.

In group therapy, I spoke to an empty chair, since our addict didn't come with us. I told the chair how much I loved him, and I thanked the chair for showing me how to be a mother. My own mother, in a different therapy group, yelled at her empty chair and said later by the pool, "Well, I told that chair a thing or two!" She also told her group, "I don't even understand what crystal meth is, and I watch *Breaking Bad!*"

Then one morning another mother approached me in the hotel exercise room and said, "I know you're trying hard here with your husband and your parents, but your son is not going to care that you went to family therapy."

She wasn't being mean. It was just the truth. It felt like we were like two prisoners on a chain gain of parents of addicted kids.

The last day was a grief lecture by Sister Geneva, and I didn't want to go at all, but it was so full of love and joy and light and forgiveness. Sister Geneva was so beautiful and I was crying. Afterwards I went to the bathroom to wash my face and pull it together, and when I was finished, I walked out and ran straight into Sister Geneva. And she saw my face and she grabbed me and held me so tightly and said, "You have loved someone so much and isn't that a wonderful thing?"

Eventually, Calvin went to rehab and relapsed and went to rehab and relapsed and went to…and so on. And my tears became so boring. You again? And the shame of being a bad mother was something I couldn't shake. Somebody told me to find an object that represented all the feelings I had about being a bad mother. My friend advised me to find this object because that way I could look at the object and recognize that these were just feelings and put them down.

And so, I found my bad mother object. It was bone—a large cow bone femur from the Tennessee farm that the kids found on a vacation visiting my husband's family when they were little. They'd gone on a bone hunt as explorers with their cousins and come back ecstatic with treasures.

That big family intervention was over six years ago. I used to watch my son from behind a kind of giant aquarium. Actually, he was in one aquarium and I was in the other. Side by side…I could check his Facebook status. *Active one hour ago. Active one day ago.* He might have posted an Instagram of himself tightrope walking a bridge in downtown L.A. Then abruptly he closed down his Instagram account. We've

unfriended and blocked each other countless times on
Facebook.

Where are you now, Calvin? Have you forgotten us? When
you show up in your hurricane suit, storming up the street,
a chorus of furies, yanking up tomato stakes as you yell, "En
guard! En guard! Take that and that!"

Have you forgotten me, my boy? When you fall on the
couch only to rise four days later refreshed and ready for the
fight to begin again?

Smashed chairs, broken cups, a spray of cereal—addiction
porn, that's what this is.

What did he do now, bless your heart?

Have you forgotten everything, my boy?

Do you remember the day we rode razor scooters to the
movies and stuck them under the seats? Do you remember the
day we looked for dinosaurs behind the secret steps of Silver
Lake? Do you remember when we made those awful donuts
from the Elvis cookbook, *Are You Hungry Tonight*? Hard as
stones, we threw them like baseballs into the garden. Do you
remember when we substituted rock salt for regular salt while
making chocolate chip cookies, since we had no salt in the
house, and we thought maybe it would work, but we watched
people flinch when they took a bite? Do you remember how
we called flour "winter" when mixing the cookie dough?
Because, after all, what did you, a Southern California boy,
know of winter? When it was time to add flour, you said, "Let
me pour in winter, Mama. It's my turn to pour in winter!"

Later, much later, winter came and stayed even on the
hottest of L.A. days.

I held and rocked Calvin every day as a baby in that studio
apartment on Valentino Place in Hollywood. His father wore
him in a baby sling and danced with him. We sang and laughed
and stomped the wild rumpus when I read him *Where the
Wild Things Are*. In those days, Valentino's ghost roamed the
hallways, and Aphrodite lived upstairs.

I mostly manage the ache of missing someone who is here but not here. Who walks the earth and lives and breathes, but I can't call Calvin because he doesn't live anywhere in particular and he can't hang on to a phone. My father loves his grandson, but my father now has dementia that is progressing, and it's like he and Calvin are on parallel train tracks on some distant railroad, and no matter how much I think or wish or contrive, I can't figure out a way to make those parallel tracks come together one more time.

Sometimes, I want to say: *Haven't we had enough of this?* But how many times must I learn that it does no good to ask these questions? So, whenever possible, I hug our grown girls a little closer, because they miss their brother, too, and they long for him to be a brother again. One of his sisters just got married, and her brother's chair was empty at her wedding. This would have once seemed unfathomable. Relatives and friends looked for him in pictures and inquired—*was that him I saw dancing?*

No, it wasn't him you saw dancing. But I try not to think about those things.

Instead, I hold my husband's hand and we go for a walk and look at trees, or I bake a pie or make a wish or write a story to somehow reclaim our lives. Sometimes, I tell myself that our boy is on location on a film shoot far away. But then I remember that somewhere on the West Coast our boy, now a man, still lives and walks and breathes and dances and sings and tells stories and bathes in buckets and sleeps under trees.

But, maybe?

One day, like Max from *Where the Wild Things Are*, he'll find his way home.

Ann Fisher-Wirth

Postcard of an Anonymous Wooden Carving

Oh child, the heft of you in her lap,
sit bones grinding into her, little toes
extending from your stiff carved robes,
orb with the cross in one hand,
other hand raised in benediction.
Your overlarge head and mild wide eyes.
Her hands poised to embrace you,
here you are calm, in this narrow alcove,
as you both gaze into eternity. Suffering
is not yet. A light pours down around you
and around her. When you scramble
from her lap, run outside and see
if the peaches are ripening on the trees,
see if the lambs in the fields skip sideways.

Contributors

Lana K. W. Austin is the author of the novel *Like Light, Like Music* (West Virginia University Press, 2020). Her poems and short stories have been featured in *Mid-American Review, Sou'wester , Columbia Journal ,* and elsewhere. Winner of the 2019 Alabama State Poetry Society Book of the Year Award for *Blood Harmony* (Iris Press) and the 2018 Words & Music Poetry Award, Austin has an MFA from George Mason University. She teaches creative writing and composition at the University of Alabama in Huntsville.

Erin Adair-Hodges is the author of *Let's All Die Happy*, winner of the Agnes Lynch Starrett Poetry Prize. A professor of creative writing at the University of Central Missouri, she's the co-editor of *Pleiades.*

Francesca Bell is an American poet and translator. Her work appears widely in journals such as *New Ohio Review, North American Review, Massachusetts Review, Mid-American Review,* and *Prairie Schooner.* She lives with her family in Novato, California. She is the author of *Bright Stain* (Red Hen Press, 2019).

Virginia Bell is the author of *From the Belly* (Sibling Rivalry Press 2012). Her poetry is forthcoming in *riverSedge: A Journal of Art & Literature* and has appeared in *Kettle Blue Review, Hypertext Review, Fifth Wednesday Journal, Rogue Agent, Gargoyle, Cider Press Review, Spoon River Poetry Review, Poet Lore,* and other journals and anthologies. Bell is a Senior Editor with *RHINO Poetry* and teaches at Loyola University Chicago. You can learn more about her work at her website: www.virginia-bell.com.

Lauren Camp is the author of four poetry collections, most recently *Turquoise Door* (3: A Taos Press, 2018). Her third book, *One Hundred Hungers* (Tupelo Press, 2016), won the Dorset Prize and was a finalist for the Arab American Book Award and the Housatonic Book Award. Lauren's poems have appeared in *The Los Angeles Review, Slice, Sixth Finch, Terrain. org, New England Review, The Cortland Review*, and elsewhere. An emeritus fellow of the Black Earth Institute, she lives and teaches in New Mexico. You can learn more on her website at www.laurencamp.com.

Susan Taylor Chehak is a graduate of the University of Iowa Writers Workshop and the author of several novels, including *The Great Disappointment, Smithereens, The Story of Annie D.*, and *Harmony*. Her most recent publications include two collections of short stories, *This Is That* and *It's Not about the Dog*. Susan has taught fiction writing in the low residency MFA programs at Antioch University, Los Angeles, the UCLA Extension Writers' Program, the University of Southern California, and the Summer Writing Festival at the University of Iowa. She grew up in Cedar Rapids, Iowa, has spent a lot of time in Los Angeles, lives occasionally in Toronto, and at present calls Colorado home.

Leigh Anne Couch published *Houses Fly Away*, her first collection, with Zone 3 Press, as well as poems in many magazines including *PANK, Pleiades, Gulf Coast, Subtropic, Smartish Pace*, and *Cincinnati Review*. Her work has been featured in *Verse Daily*, Dzanc's *Best of the Web*, and in *The Echoing Green: Poems of Fields, Meadows, and Grasses* (Penguin). Now a freelance editor, she was formerly an editor at Duke University Press and the *Sewanee Review*. She lives in Sewanee, Tennessee with writer Kevin Wilson and their sons, Griff and Patch.

Natasha Deonarain lives part-time between Arizona and Colorado. Her poems can be found in *NELLE, Rigorous,*

Packingtown Review, Thin Air Magazine, Dime Show Review, Prometheus Dreaming, and *Canyon Voices Literary Magazine.*

Jessie LaFrance Dunbar specializes in nineteenth and twentieth century African American and African Diasporic literatures; she has secondary interests in Russian and AfroCuban history, literature, and cultures. Her current book project, *Democracy, Diaspora, and Disillusionment: Black Itinerancy and the Propaganda Wars,* suggests that scholars recalibrate the earliest notable era of Russian influence on African American politics from the twentieth century to the nineteenth century. She has published articles in journals, such as *Multiethnic Literature of the US* and *Interdisciplinary Literary Studies* as well as in *Critical Insights: Civil Rights Literature, Past & Present* and *Routledge Companion to American Literary Journalism.*

Ann Fisher-Wirth's sixth book of poems, *The Bones of Winter Birds,* was published earlier this year by Terrapin Books. Her fifth book, *Mississippi* (Wings Press 2018), is a poetry / photography collaboration with acclaimed Delta photographer Maude Schuyler Clay. Ann is co-editor, with Laura-Gray Street, of *The Ecopoetry Anthology* (Trinity UP 2013). Her work has received numerous awards. She has had residencies at Djerassi, Hedgebrook, The Mesa Refuge, and CAMAC (France) and senior Fulbright awards to Switzerland and Sweden. A senior fellow of the Black Earth Institute, she was 2017 Anne Spencer Poet in Residence at Randolph College, Virginia. She teaches at the University of Mississippi, where she also directs the Environmental Studies minor—and she teaches yoga in Oxford, MS. Her website is annfisherwirth.com.

Diamond Forde is a PhD candidate at Florida State University. Her debut book, *Mother Body,* was selected by Patricia Smith for the Saturnalia Poetry Prize and will be forthcoming in Spring 2021. She is a *Callaloo* and *Tin House* fellow. She is a recipient of the Margaret Walker Memorial Prize in Poetry.

Her work was selected as a finalist for the *Georgia Poetry Prize* and has appeared in *Ninth Letter, Tupelo Quarterly, Tinderbox Journal, The Offing*, and elsewhere.

Kate Hanson Foster's first book of poems, *Mid Drift*, was published by Loom Press and was a finalist for the Massachusetts Center for the Book Award in 2011. Her work has appeared or is forthcoming in *Birmingham Poetry Review, Comstock Review, Harpur Palate, Poet Lore, Salamander, Tupelo Quarterly*, and elsewhere. In 2017, she was awarded the NEA Parent Fellowship through the Vermont Studio Center. She lives and writes in Groton, Massachusetts.

Jennifer Habel Jennifer Habel is the author of *Good Reason,* winner of the Stevens Poetry Manuscript Competition, and *The Book of Jane*, winner of the Iowa Poetry Prize. Her recent work has appeared in *Alaska Quarterly Review, The Common, Denver Quarterly, Mid-American Review, Pleiades*, and *The Sewanee Review*.

Rachel Hall is the author of *Heirlooms* (BkMk Press), which was selected by Marge Piercy for the G.S. Sharat Chandra book prize. *Heirlooms* was also the winner of the Phillip McMath post publication prize and runner up for the Edward Lewis Wallant Prize. Hall's stories and essays have been published in a number of journals, including *Bellingham Review, Gettysburg Review, Natural Bridge*, and *Guernica*. She has received honors and awards from *Glimmer Train, Lilith, New Letters*, the Bread Loaf and Sewanee Writers' Conferences, Ragdale, and Ox-Bow School of the Arts. She is Professor of English at SUNY Geneseo.

Lisa Beech Hartz directs Seven Cities Writers Project, a non-profit bringing cost-free creative writing workshops to underserved communities. She currently guides workshops in a city jail and an LGBT community center. Her ekphrastic collection, *The Goldfish Window*, was published by Grayson Books in 2018.

Abriana Jetté is the editor of the *Stay Thirsty Poets* anthology series and Editor-in-Chief at Rove-Over Books in addition to writing poetry and creative nonfiction. She currently lives in New Jersey, where she is a Lecturer in Writing Studies at Kean University.

Carrie La Seur is a recovering environmental lawyer and author of two award-winning, critically acclaimed novels from William Morrow: *The Home Place* (2014) and *The Weight of an Infinite Sky* (2018). Her poetry, short stories, essays, book reviews, and law review articles appear in *The Guardian*, *Harvard Law and Policy Review*, *Inscape*, *Kenyon Review*, *Mother Jones*, *Rappahannock Review*, *Rumpus*, *Salon*, and more. She lives in Montana.

Sandy Longhorn has received the Porter Fund Literary Prize for Arkansas authors and the Collins Prize from the *Birmingham Poetry Review*. She is the author of three books of poetry: *The Alchemy of My Mortal Form, The Girlhood Book of Prairie Myths,* and *Blood Almanac*. Her poems have appeared in *The Cincinnati Review*, *Hayden's Ferry Review*, *North American Review*, *Oxford American*, *Thrush*, and elsewhere. Longhorn teaches in the Arkansas Writers MFA program at the University of Central Arkansas, where she directs the C.D. Wright Women Writers Conference.

Angie Macri is the author of *Underwater Panther* (Southeast Missouri State University), winner of the Cowles Poetry Book Prize, and *Fear Nothing of the Future or the Past* (Finishing Line). Her recent work appears in *American Literary Review*, *New England Review*, and *Tupelo Quarterly*. An Arkansas Arts Council fellow, she lives in Hot Springs.

Kerry Madden is the author of a new picture book, *Ernestine's Milky Way*, published by Schwartz & Wade of Random House and selected as the State Book of Alabama at the National Book Festival in Washington, D.C. She wrote the Smoky Mountain Trilogy for children, which includes *Gentle's Holler*, *Louisiana's Song*, and *Jessie's Mountain*, published by Viking. Her first novel, *Offsides* (Morrow), was a New York Public Library Pick for the Teen Age. Her book *Up Close Harper Lee* made Booklist's Ten Top Biographies of 2009 for Youth. She also wrote *Writing Smarts* published by American Girl, filled story sparks to encourage young writers. Her first picture book, *Nothing Fancy About Kathryn and Charlie*, was illustrated by her daughter, Lucy, and published by Mockingbird Publishers. Kerry is a regular contributor to the *Los Angeles Times* OpEd Page. She directs the Creative Writing Program at the University of Alabama at Birmingham and teaches in the Antioch MFA Program in Los Angeles. The mother of three adult children, she divides her time between Birmingham and Los Angeles.

Jennifer Martelli is the author of *My Tarantella* (Bordighera Press), awarded an Honorable Mention from the Italian-American Studies Association and selected as a 2019 "Must Read" by the Massachusetts Center for the Book. Her chapbook, *After Bird*, was the winner of the Grey Book Press open reading, 2016. Her work is forthcoming in *Poetry Magazine* and *The Sycamore Review* and, most recently, has appeared in *Verse Daily*, *The DMQ Review*, *The Sonora Review*, and *Iron Horse Review* (winner, Photo Finish contest). Jennifer Martelli is the recipient of the Massachusetts Cultural Council Grant in Poetry. She is co-poetry editor for *Mom Egg Review* and co-curates the Italian-American Writers Series at I AM Books in Boston.

Michelle McMillan-Holifield is a recent Best of the Net and Pushcart Prize nominee. Her work has been included in or is forthcoming in *Boxcar Poetry Review, Jabberwock Review, Sky Island Journal, Sleet Magazine, Stirring, The Collagist, Toasted Cheese, Whale Road Review*, and *Windhover*, among others. She hopes you one day find her poetry tacked to a tree somewhere in the Alaskan Wild.

Sandra Meek has published six books of poems, including *Still* (Persea, January 2020), *An Ecology of Elsewhere, Road Scatter*, and the Dorset Prize-winning *Biogeography*. Recipient of an NEA Fellowship in Poetry, the Poetry Society of America's Lucille Medwick Memorial Award, three Georgia Author of the Year awards, and two Peace Corps Writers awards, she is co-founding editor of Ninebark Press, director of the Georgia Poetry Circuit, poetry editor of the *Phi Kappa Phi Forum*, and Dana Professor of English, Rhetoric, and Writing at Berry College. Visit her at www.sandrameek.com.

Amanda Moore's poetry has appeared in journals and anthologies including *ZZYZVA, Cream City Review, Tahoma Literary Review*, and *Best New Poets*, and she is the recipient of writing awards from The Writing Salon, Brush Creek Arts Foundation, and The Saltonstall Foundation for the Arts. Amanda is a high school teacher and lives by the beach in the Outer Sunset neighborhood of San Francisco with her husband and daughter. You can learn more about her work at amandapmoore.com.

Alison Pelegrin is the author of four poetry collections, most recently *Waterlines* (LSU Press). The recipient of fellowships from the National Endowment for the Arts and the Louisiana Division of the Arts, her work has appeared in *Tin House, The Bennington Review, Poetry East,* and *The Southern Review.*

Charlotte Pence's first book of poems, *Many Small Fires* (Black Lawrence Press, 2015), received an INDIEFAB Book of the Year Award from Foreword Reviews. She is also the author of two award-winning poetry chapbooks and the editor of *The Poetics of American Song Lyrics*. Her poetry, fiction, and creative nonfiction have been published in *Harvard Review, Sewanee Review, Southern Review,* and *Brevity*. She is the director of the Stokes Center for Creative Writing at the University of South Alabama. Her next book, *Code,* is forthcoming May of 2020.

Catherine Esposito Prescott is the author of the chapbooks *Maria Sings* and *The Living Ruin*. Recent poems have appeared in *Bellevue Literary Review, Flyway, MiPOesias, Pleiades, Poetry East, Southern Poetry Review, South Florida Poetry Journal,* and *TAB: The Journal of Poetry & Poetics,* as well as the anthologies *99 Poets for the 99 Percent* and *The Orison Anthology*. Prescott earned an MFA in Creative Writing from NYU. She is a co-founder of SWWIM, which curates a reading series in Miami Beach and publishes the online literary journal *SWWIM Every Day*.

Debra Eubanks Riffe is a native of Tupelo, Mississippi, and earned her BFA from Howard University's College of Fine Arts in Washington, D.C. She has been a professional graphic designer and illustrator for more than thirty years. Debra has traveled extensively and lived in Barranquilla, Colombia, for five years. Her studio practice is, exclusively, hand-printed relief prints of woodcuts and linoleum blocks. The juxtaposition of a doily and silhouette are familiar shapes in her prints and are reflective of her signature style. Her narrative titles and bold, realistic depictions of working-class individuals are fundamental components in representing African Americans as a primary theme. Debra is a member of a Birmingham, AL, printmaking cooperative and teaches linoleum block relief printmaking workshops, locally and regionally, twice a year. Additionally, she is a printmaking instructor with Auburn University's Alabama Prison Arts + Education Project (APAEP), directed by Kyes Stevens.

Jess Smith is currently a PhD candidate in English at Texas Tech University in Lubbock, Texas, where she co-founded and curates the LHUCA Literary Series. Her work can be found in *Prairie Schooner, Waxwing, 32 Poems, The Rumpus,* and other journals. She received her MFA in poetry from The New School and is the recipient of support from the Sewanee Writers' Conference and the Vermont Studio Center.

Katrina Smolinsky is a poet from the Olympic Peninsula. She is an MFA in Poetry candidate at the College of Charleston and a graduate of The Evergreen State College. She can be found on Twitter @KatSmolinsky.

Lynne Thompson is the author of *Start with A Small Guitar* (What Books Press, 2015) and *Beg No Pardon* (Perugia Press, 2007). She is a winner of the Great Lakes Colleges Association's New Writers Award. Her latest manuscript, *Fretwork,* won the 2018 Marsh Hawk Press Poetry Prize and was published in 2019. Recent work appears or is forthcoming in *Poetry, Ploughshares, Pleiades, New England Review,* and *Black Renaissance Noire.*

Jessica Turney was raised in Madera, California, and graduated with her MFA in Poetry from Fresno State. She worked for *The Normal School Literary Magazine* and the *San Joaquin Review* as a managing and poetry editor. She has been published in *A Sharp Piece of Awesome* and was a finalist in *Frontier's* OPEN prize. She also received the Ernesto Trejo Poetry Prize from the Academy of American Poets. Jessica currently resides in the Central Valley with her cat, Minerva.